Laminations

Laminations

by
Page Nelson

© Copyright 2016 Page Nelson

The author asserts his moral right not to be identified as the author of this work.

Any reproduction, re-printing, etc., without express permission is strictly permitted.

This is a work of friction. Names, places, events, etc. are either the products of the author's imagination or are abused in a fictitious manner. Historical figures, persons of notoriety or persons likely to become so may appear in settings and/or imaginary actions indicative or depictive of actual events.

The author is a legally incorporated entity in the Talau Federation. By reading this statement, you agree to participate in an aesthetic activity and to release, waive, discharge, and covenant not to sue, and agree to hold the author, his assigns, co-signs, legatees, and companion animals from and against any and all liabilities, demands, claims, damages or injuries, including death, that you may sustain during or in conjunction with this activity.

As attested in articles on file in the Commonwealth of Virginia, all profits are designated to animal welfare.

ISBN: 978-1-941066-14-0

Cataloging-at-Publication Data

Nelson, Page, 1952-

Laminations / by Page Nelson.

   1. Aphorisms American – 21st century – Biography 2. Aphorisms and apothegms 3. American poetry – 21st century.

| II. Title. | 2016.RDA-NEG8 |
| PN6271.N443 2016 | CAP/NOTCIP |

Catalogued to pre-2014 conventions in conformity with standards approved by the American Association of Cataloging Rules Conservation (AACRC).

Credits. Epigrams: Adorno, translated by Robert Hullot-Kentor; Rabbat, translated by J. Hopkinds; Rilke, translated by Ulrich Baer and adapted by the author; book design by Jo-Anne Rosen; back cover art, *Laminations IV* by Guy Mantis, courtesy of the Lickiser Gallery, New York.

The power of subjectivity in late works of art is the irascible gesture with which it takes leave of the works themselves. Late works are catastrophes.
— Theodor Adorno

It is proper to thanks one's teachers in order of the value of their instruction; first one's parents, then one's betrayers, then all other sensei. — Roshi Rabbat

Everything that others forget in order to make life possible, artists constantly strive to uncover and enlarge; we actually awaken monsters which we have no intention of killing. We are attracted to them, they posses power. It is not our role to make ourselves tamers of our inner lions. But suddenly, we find ourselves marching alongside them as if in a triumphal procession, without any recollection of the moment of this inconceivable reconciliation. An ever so slightly sloped bridge links what is terrible to what is gentle. — Rainer Marie Rilke, letter to Baladine Klossowska (Nov.18,1920)

Das ganz vollendete und vollkommne Verstehen selbst aber ... [The entirely complete and perfect understanding itself, however...] — last words (written) of the suddenly dying Friedrich Schlegel.

Introduction

Laminations is the last of my experiments in "literary mixed media". It is composed of four elements: a reader's/writer's (more the former than the latter) journal of four months' intermittent extent, a small gathering of poems selected from my prior publications, a more sizable compilation of aphorisms, comprising both old and new work and finally, a short "anthology" of poems generously contributed to the project by friends and benefactors.

There is no feature or functionality of constitutive identity about the elements, their presentation as one aesthetic object being essentially an act of categorical will which does not preclude a congenial or susceptible reader supplying via his or her individual phenomenology of reading the missing or only inchoately absent features that would constitute an organic whole.

By far the hardest component to contrive was what would seem easiest, the journal, each entry being an unreflective recordation of fragments of the writer's day. Unreflective, yes, but what to leave in, leave out, with the burden too of knowing this was nowhere near art, even bad art, lacking then its powers of structural self-enablement, when I have never thought my daily activity worthy of mine or anyone else's special attention. Going over such a text again for minimal proofreading, since composition itself is the initial act of reading, was a significantly testing task. What could be the justification of its unremediated presentment to any other person? Only this: it seemed, here, without pre or post mediation, raw not cooked, was the stark presentation of a mind in mundane mental activity (where minds, most themselves, generally operate), one man's track thoughts, an individual texture, not remotely as entertaining or significant as Pepys' yet like his in its distinctive daily taint. "This I was" – with no insinuation that the emergent "me" or its documentation would be appealing.

The poetry in the second section, selected from four self-published chapbooks, represents a small part of my not large body of work and not necessarily the best of it. But the somewhat distancing historical themes, deliberately crafted to project a focal point beyond the self, seemed a corrective complement to the personality of the "rough" journal. Bibliographers will certainly need to know that in two brief exposures, in my late twenties and early sixties, I did attempt to objectively publish my work in "real" journals (how real they were or how valid the process of their adjudication is, as all rejected writers know, decidedly problematic), submitting approximately fifty-five submission packets to magazine, resulting in four acceptances and subsequent appearances in print (laude *Blue Lantern*, *Writer's Eye*, *Antiphon* and *Fiddler Crab*), an acceptance rate of about seven or eight percent that was not enough to encourage me to attempt to increase it. It is curious to realize that in the United Kingdom, this result would incontestably qualify me, by objective Home Office formulated standards, as an "identified poet", eligible for retirement in The Royal Hoar Poets' Home (Chelsea), with its life-enhancing ambience of good cheer and rota of wholesome activities such as bingo bouts with the boisterous old soldiers just up the road.*

---

* Team bingo, called "Jingo", featuring bridge like competitive bidding on held cards ("hands"), is a popular geriatric pastime in the United Kingdom.

Here, in the harshly Darwinian valenced US of A, I'm left to sourly sequestrate in this subversive (too many weeds, too vigorous) suburban garden, reciting my imperfectly remembered stanzos to the couldn't care less air, alone but for the scruffy squirrels that stagger up in their characteristic passive-aggressive stop-start, hop(p)ing, too insistently for a nut. A sad fate for even a seven percent poet. But you are wondering, do I satisfy the importunate, cosmetically semi-arboreal rodents at a higher rate than the editors did me? Yes, there is a rough justice in the world, (c)hew it how we will – only rough. There was too a darker purpose behind *Lamination's* poetic layering.

All motivations are embodied in method and the mentor of mine was Field Marshal Bernard Law ("Monty") Montgomery, specifically his planning for the Goodwood attacks in Normandy, July 1944. Rather than detail the tactical maneuvers, the bustling business of many current histories, I will give an overall operational abstract and explanation of its relevance to the work in hand. A blocking defensive position may be so strong that the attacker, whom we shall call "Monty", despairs of making an all out, direct assault that will likely fail or succeed only at prohibitive coast. He conceives another way. A significant attack *is* launched, with artillery and infantry that causes fall back in the defenders, who perforce, bring in reinforcements, including armor (tanks), from reserves and other parts of their line. In this state of limited success, the attacker, whose goal for reasons cited was not in fact break through, begins an orderly retreat back over the front of his recent advance. The defenders, strengthened and committed in force at the face of contact, sense weakness and mount a counterattack. Attacker and defender have changed roles with the crucial factor being that the original defenders have weakened their line on either flank and are forward from their best defensive position. It is at then that "Monty" launches a major flank attack with his uncommitted armor and reserves to achieve a decisive breakthrough, a method that has been called "grapple and strike." In *Laminations*, the lumbering attack is embodied in the journal entries, which encumbers the reader with low-order, fatiguing prosaic elements that are persistent and plentiful. The opposing lexical infantry commits itself, losing verbal mobility and resistant powers. It is at that point of embedded arrow vulnerability that the poetry appears, in highly developed, concise, metaphorically charged assault. The resulting "breakthroughs" are followed up and consolidated by mobile but penetrative aphoristic elements ("saws"), with final cleanup of redoubt and command holdouts assigned to the specialized teams of contributor poetry. The reader is left reeling, in headlong retreat from his prepared positions. This is the overall operational strategy (alternatively, a physics of successive accessibilities and resistancies) of *Laminations*. Indeed the book might have been named Goodwood but for the signified timber being bitten, blasted, knotted, dried and warped, not good wood at all. All that I, honest logman, have to hew. As to concerns that anterior transparency might mitigate the trope's latter effectiveness, studies conducted at Edmister University's Institute for Textual Studies (ITS) have shown divergent and distinct areas of cerebral activity as indicated by glucosive illumination associatively co-coordinated with subject's exclusive exposure to poetry or prose while undergoing MRI. This is *not* to propound a theory of bio-aestheticism. We have no coherent account, not one, of what aesthetic experience is excepting along the most accessible social-political lines where Adorno is still leader of the pack. We are left with *vita brevis, ars longa* which might (must) mean more than its commonplace registration of the relative longevity of disparate ("desperate"? –ed) objects in time. Since our lives (vitae) are self-perceived, to suppose they are short compared to the length and the extension in depth of our aesthetic experiences that are in time but not of time (and given this might be so of all our experiences), is to problematically privilege the artistic and return us to the invalid condition of aesthetic theory. For creators and appreciators of art, a conundrum. As is that everyday problematic or miracle or illusion – that somehow we (ourselves composites) perceive "wholes" in a composition of parts. Which is the vital vision, like a momentary and knowing sidelong glance engendering these laminations that may yet, for all their mega rather than micro dimensionality resolve into a unity, appreciable in parts whose appropriate amplitudes are valedictory and belated.

[Of course, an introduction is an observation post from which the work is viewed across a chasm of self-alienation. Significant features, if they are not mirages, may be seen but the actual texture of terrain can only be touched by *traversement*. So much for introductions.]

Journal

"The question here refers less to the knowledge of the truth than to the knowledge of verisimilitude. An event may not have occurred despite the allegations of the chronicler. But the fact that the author could have stated such an event is at least as interesting as the simple occurrence of an event simply proceeding from chance. When an author is mistaken or lying, his text is no less significant than when he is conveying 'the truth.'"

– Tzvetan Todorov, *The Conquest of America*

The journal that follows was maintained for four months, with an entry or two a week, between Sept. 8 and Dec.30, 2016. As there is very little causal or narrative connection between entries, each day being its own boundary, it seemed misleading to present them in straight chronological order whereby the reader, in the natural act of reading, imposes a continuity that does not, in itself, exist. Preventively then, the daily segments (now numbered) have been published in a randomized arrangement. Anyone wishing to reconstruct the order of composition order can do so noting the number at the end of each segment, finding and reading the next segment thus designated, proceedingly. It can't be overemphasized that this is writing "as it happens", with little consideration for continuity or craft, best apprehended by scansion and skippery. (The reader, decisively addressed as integral to the construction, is a definitely identified abstraction amiably advised to peruse no more than two or three diary entries (the journal being not a prerequisite but a pre-condition) before proceeding to the poetry section for a single poem, concluding with one page of aphorisms, a series of repeatable "rounds" or "developments" best presenting the work's laminous flavor.)

Editorial note. Aside from spatial and typographical conforming, the journal is reproduced exactly as stored on the 32GB red plastic (with white Harvard University signa VE-RI-TAS) USB drive housed in the Small Special Collections Library at the University of Virginia (accession number 37934867D), without editorial interventions or corrections.

---

1. Sept. 8   Reading the last of Virginia Woolf's diaries – she's on the way out after riding the two rough waves of *The Waves* and *The Years*, a burnout case with that haunted, not yet diagnosed cancer look: what's left – ashes and the final "between the acts" that isn't – curtains. I used to love her, love desiccated now to a neat little sachet packet of sowed up, tucked-in admiration/respect. Yes, pace Larkin, love dies, is annihilated every day. Yet her diary, like any perusal of ruins (or remains of the day) is poignant and of interest, the daily revelation of a life.

My personal literary declension (a cunning to be strange[1]) has been from ambitious novel to intense poetry to aphorism to this mundane recordation. Well, literature itself is dead, dead, that is, as formerly conceived and under currently prevailing conditions, assailed by the enticements of interactive multimedia(the iPhone is more exactly the *I Phone*, an identity not a brand) and facile "feel good" aesthetical politics – the last generation to whom it mattered in the high canonical sense, was, well, mine allowing

---

1   The alternate title of this collection, from Romeo and Juliette (2.2.102-105)."But trust me, gentleman, I'll prove more true /Than those that have more cunning to be strange."

for those 15 years younger like "Paul"² (not perhaps his false name) still captivated by texts even if only as necessary precursors to mastitising theory, feeding on the host body to the point of exhaustion though to call it the cancer of the conceptual is unfair. What matters now, screen writing (stories, novels mere raw (maw?) material for the visual (albeit purely visually conceived videos are almost nonexistent except as "media" art exhibits, the true living dead, flickering in vacant galleries, Soho), the endless exasperations of popular music that still require a lyric. Literature is sensorially deprived. Why, in an era with no respect for hierarchy (and when real power is masked and when "aesthetic" means "elitist"), would anyone submit to an author? As to the novel, it is the academy painting of our era, with its suite of schooled techniques (purveyed by creative writing programs), false to life in trying to be artful and false to art trying to be lifelike.³

---

2   A brilliant theoretical mind whose works remained theoretical.

3   Wilde is harsher, "Anyone can write a novel. It merely requires complete ignorance of both life and literature." My own dicta usually have an arch tone that is their built-in qualification, the reaching too far overtone itself a reservation. In Wilde's defense, *his* most overweening pronouncements (op. cit.) are spoken by characters. The ideal modern novel would be a mystical marriage of Beckett's magnificent monologic mumbles with any good English writer's (Powell or Tolkien) fluent tale spinning. Kafka comes closest but rhetorical oil seldom mixes with narrative vinegar. In the case in hand, a kind of in-the-same-room frankness is interlaced with threads of qualitative and quantitative verbal complexity. My personal ideal novel— a short primary text of thirty pages with an extensive set of footnotes that generates footnotes until the fourth generation of notes generates a set that is ... the original text, backwards. I believe only one writer in the world has the skill to pull this feat off, the Franco-Senegalese author Adda Oulipo, to whom I would humbly suggest the title *A Quintessence of Dust*.

Instead of killing books, computers proliferated them by many millions thanks to software assisted printing which in turn led to inexpensive methods of self-publication. Literature became little different from a blog, a thing utterly democratic, one dimensional and non-aesthetic. The rare good result has been that literature has become so commonplace and poetry, in particular, so prosaic, we have, unless we are studious and antiquarian, "forgotten the moves" in the aesthetic game so that however jaded, every now and again, one is freakishly moved and astonished by an effective poem, The vast plain of ignorable writing, traversed by inept readers, has cleared the vista for that rare promontory – a poem that works.[4] Of course, it really is all downhill and, as every generation discovers, always has been only now the de-gradation is steeper than ever,[5] "Belatedness" being ever new. "Kids today." Such dicta are "always already", of interest only as points, places of departure and in this case I am bold to say, not even that. I am going on too long, but the definition of literature as "verbal over-determination" allows me to prove if not proof my pedigree. My own latter day successes in genre: letters to the editor; 2 to *The Economist*, 3 to the *LRB* (4 by the time you read this, the most amusing of which was[6]), 7 in

---

4 The situation is not new. "Lots of poetry, few poems." – Friedrich Schlegel (1772-1829).

5 The basic rule is clear enough, the broader the interconnectivity, the shallower the language. "Wasup?| Reading|?| war/peace |wow|luvAndre|me2|kool.|joke|Ino." (see D. Donoghue, T*he Defeat of Poetry*.)

6 "Dear Editors, Readers persuaded by Robert Potts' lucid argument (LRB, 2 June) that J.H. Prynne's poetry is more than an emperor's new clothes phenomenon may wish to apply their improved powers of appreciation to the recent work of A.T. Random whose poem

the *TLS*, 2 in *Private Eye*.[7] These need to be added to my archive in UVa "Special Collections", that Small, funeral parlor resembling underground library designed by the finest Dutch engineers, your water being a grave corrupter of the corpuses (a subterranean pun if there ever was one) and – not bad (my archive I mean) for a boy born on a mountaintop in Tennessee (best advice you may ever be given: never stop at a bar in Tennessee unless you relish a brawl), reared amid the sweepings of the Norfolk (Va.) broomdocks. Bubble and squeak, tasting the tang, even a mile inland, of the sea. Nashville's particularly American sonic brew of uncultivated and flaunted self-pity was not for me. (My self-pity being, if nothing else, cultivated, a pearl of pathos wherein I palely see myself.)

I retire from making art, having produced four chapbooks of poetry and four not large volumes of "literary mixed media." (Joyce of course, was, in his admixtures, was still producing "lit"—how derby hat dated was that? I am presenting litter, collage, being the first person in my family to be collage educated. At what quantum split was that funny?) It's not exactly the case that I no longer believe in art but I don't believe in any further advancement of

---

"Every Twentieth Word of Potts' Review" begins, *"It to no he synonymous, his fear spreading pitch, Sampson society./ Again this gave to symbolic, perversely, past practice ..."* (Random, being a poet, may have lost exact word count here and there. Punctuation supplied.) Yours truly, Page Nelson." Two weeks later, the LRB emailed me to say mine was 'the 25th funniest letter they had ever decided not to print" and that given they only publish 10% of the 200 letters they receive bi-weekly, I should feel gratified.

7   The British satirical magazine."Harder for Americans to get in than *The Economist.*", according to *Foreign Affiars*.

MY art, referring any remnants of appreciators (Ausonius? Huhee?) to the vast reservoir of already existing great art to draw upon, a good market for the consumer. Crediting THAT, I commence my aesthetic retirement. After all, my personal passion is spent and art without passion is what? Doodling arabesquing, shrunk shanking, professional posturings, prayers without thoughts never to heaven going – much of what we see in contemporary literature – obligatory professional poses (including the performatory experimental, i.e. Jorie Grahamism), which even if competent (Is Graham competent? Who could tell?), exhibits practice without belief. Goings through (e)motions. Or worse –Ashburyings. To be interred under heaps of light weight, grey floccules, a rug of smug; there's nothing substantive to shake off yet it suffocates. Trash bury. Oh, he's cool alright, cool if he could go like a crab backwards to when men wore suites and proper ladies little snail shell hats with veils.

You might consider this a helluva beginning. We've enough old men not going gentle into their good nights. (Reminding me of "A hell**UVA**school" – a bumptious promotional bumper sticker for the University of Virginia, UVa, that perennially crass place where I expended my spirit in a waste of shame, where any night these last 150 years, you could leave the library and run into a huddle of spewing frat boys or come across a spunky probationary, bound and naked, dry humping a street light. As a real beginning, may I offer this translation of my favorite Rilke poem:

Late Autumn in Venice

The city no longer drifts like a lure

catching the surfacing days.

Glassy palaces ring brittle

against the passing glance.

In the gardens, summer like a heap of marionettes,

hangs head down, unstrung, broken.

But out of the ground, from bosky skeletons,

The Will rises, as if overnight

the sea's commendatore had multiplied

galleys in the wakeful arsenal,

pitched into the morning breeze

a fleet setting out, stately rowing,

that catching the wind, flags rippling,

is suddenly radiant and dire.

(For grammatical assistance and for a sense of Rilke's general tone, I am indebted to the masterful translations of Edward Snow. Any errors (such as that poetically dubious "suddenly" in the last line; the suddenness should be imminent and unspoken) are mine alone, excepting those due to leaping cats. That said – *The above is a copyrighted translation belonging to Page Nelson. Any publication, re-publication, duplication, replication, application, reading (including private readings), performances (public or private), storage on optical disc or other means electrical-mechanical, adaptation for stage, screen, television, game, or use, wholly or in part, in advertising, product or service promotion, event and concert publicity, including charitable promotions, without the expressed written permission of the proctors of the Page Nelson Translation Trust, (a nonprofit association organized under Title 17.1 United States Code and Article 44.8 the Federal Tax Code, co-headquartered in Charlottesville Virginia in the United States of America, and the Taulau Federation, a United Nations administered autonomous region) is expressly prohibited. Infractions are subject to compulsory adjudication under enforcement provisions that include but are not limited to incarceration, fines, restitutions, restorative indentures, public shaming, pro-se penalties, court costs, other exactions and reparations as imposed, concurrent and nonconcurrently, by EUROCAT (the European Copyright Accession Treaty) and other relevant jurisdictions, excepting exculpatory sections of the Talau Federation Declaration of Human Rights (TFDHR). Appeals: there are no appeals.*

This is actually the way I think and pass my days. Time now for my nap and yours too if you are not asleep already. [8]

2. Nov. 26 An asset of age, these intense dreams, never had when, in youthful ferment, I was incapable of deep sleep. Now, the outward reach of the sexual is reversed, inversed in intensities of a rich and erotic dreamscape. Last night the best of noctures about my first wife – no need to rehearse the old, old story. In the dream, what little I recalled of it in the long light of morning, after various complicated plots, we were alone, she never more resplendent with her honey hair, angel length, her golden Kazak eyes, her high cheeked intelligent, her look, indescribable.

I knew what had passed between us in the dream of real life, knew she knew and said "I never stopped loving you, not ever." And she said, smiling, her remark in its lightness the more weighty for the brutality that had passed between us, "I love you too. Let's go away together, they will understand." meaning whomever the anon person she was in dream real time involved with and discounting BF, implying the relation proposed was somehow allowable though I knew it was disruptive and I thought yes I will do this but BF will resist and I cannot say where this will end. Nothing explicit, it was better than sex to this extent: I've had great sex and the next hour it has no purchase, leaves no harmonic wake while this was sustained, semi-indelible, real in its force, vivacity and durability. Sweet, because a restoration, when it is genuine, has a higher reality quotient than the old reality that was always already damaged and required repair (see *A Winter's Tale*). Oh yes, perchance to dream. The thing about dreams, most of mine except this one, they lack the weight of consequence, the sense that anything that happens, matters, compelling yes, but like the catharsis induced by film, not fully enveloping because texturally thin. [5]

One morning glory did not fade in the sun,
enduring to outface the forgetful moon.

3. Oct. 16   Our brave tars, no, our clean cut lads, like the sailor jack trademark of the caramel popcorn snack, onanistically grinning in his nautical pajamas with the pup dog daemon, were never lately tars, have sailed on their brave little boat into the red seas of the evil Chang to show him he can't rule the waves. Our national identity enhancing myth (Columbia Queen of the shining seas), as theirs, showing in every textbook the sweating white brutes that stomped through the delicate summer palaces, the scented silk pavilions and willow gazebos, burning, looting, and take-a-break raping. Who can doubt this is all going to end very badly? Everybody knows it but nothing is done to prevent, the events have an inexorable, fatal logic of their own, another August 1914 reaping. Or consider the agreement on global warming, carbon addicted countries pledge, like honest alcoholics, to cut their intake, in this case output and it is nothing but a patch on conscience, a cover, so things can go on exactly as they do. The war is going to happen, the planet is going to drown because people, aside from mere complacency, have an active destructive appetite for misery and struggle. The Sino-American War, the polluted planet. Take your pick, take both.

Today I woke, smelling very badly (and to think someone has just written a book, defending Tudor hygiene, claiming she didn't bathe in three months and never smelt bad. Says who? And what time of year?) which to clarify, I was smelling pooty good for an old man but what I was detecting for the first time, I think, was a lingering, clinging odor of rot, flowers too long in the vase, something more than the, hardly noticed, usual burnt out electric cord whiff in my nostrils and true too, over the last few months, how many times I fear to recall, a persistent little whizz at the back of my throat, a cat's whine, a mouse's serenade some new bad thing (or hypochondria), tiny voices keening inevitable death. Or it could happen in an instant – not news. Your life the physics of the candle flame, lambent and illuminating as long as the right/tight physics prevail. Exhausted tallow, a wick topples, a sudden breeze puts out the light. True, we were born into this world of miracles and what may follow?[8] In the habit of living, we cannot believe we will die. Where is the cat? It was loved, it can't be no where, it must be somewhere. So describe that somewhere, make it creditable, kinda. And, faithfully, we do. [26]

Suppose the bright leaves had never fallen, withering on the trees.

4. Oct.13 It occurred to me today, chill slate day of rain, dry oak leaves beaten down in mushy ridges, that I need to really see that the world, this sharp, acid smelling earth will go on without me, be there undiminished the next second after my death. I know it but I need to understand that what I see will not be changed. As to any afterlife, why also have I not seen the obvious – it must be timeless, out of time and surely no consciousness we can think of, that might comfort us, could abide there. Time is our essential element.

On the TV news: every hot dog you eat shortens your life by 3.8 minutes. My god, I've eaten hundreds – they use to serve them in the schools, gov subsidized tubes of approved nutrition and not one was so good as to be worth 3.8 minutes of life, The TV drones on "and for those put up the butt, five minutes" my god, what did he just say?

---

8 An obvious point to be made: our knowledge is dependent on our senses and conceptual powers. Both are limited in their apprehensions, which include our capacity to understand the totality of ourselves, also objects in the world.

"five minutes of *added* life span." Scientists are not sure why (the preservatives? the thrill?) and this is only one study. "No one should read this results and start inserting processed meat between their wry buns since this addiction, association rather, the substitution of hotdogs by Italian sausages by Hebrew national salamis is a known hazard with no life benefits whatsoever." That's a relief, I guess.

Been reading Bate's ("Master" Bate, I think it is, of St. Onan's College, Oxford) big biography of Ted Hughes, so posted this online review.

"More than commendably researched and lucidly written, with fresh insights on a stale case, no doubt essential and the as yet definitive biography, still the overall effect is deadening and dull, a curiously void account of one of the most passionate male poet lives of the 20th century. We are given intelligent 'receptions' (rehashes) of Hughes beefy works, we are informed of their vital contexts, treated to a catalogue of some of his multitudinous lovers but Bate is so careful to be nonjudgmental, at a judicious remove from this over-touristed old battlefield that it all ends just another 'balanced' biographical page turner. (Assia kills herself and her kid and we go, in response to the measured narrative flow 'Oh, ok.') The book has all the well-groomed and anemic qualities of any don's well-tempered and thoroughly safe seated professional excursion, Oxbridge Tours. If one were to ask 'what alternative?' I'd say look at Janet (redbrick u.) Todd's Wollstonecraft which is morally and critically engaged (often controversially) at every life stage. Amazing the Hughes family didn't approve the book because I doubt Ted could be left-lying (yuk-yuk-yuk) to look any better. A bloke's bloke, okay? (As I was first to observe. to

lose one wife to suicide is a tragedy, to lose two begins to look like carelessness.) Compare to Middlebrook's more emotionally incisive "Her Husband." Granted Bate was handling dynamite ('Tedite', tedneedstwat= TNT), but there is too much moral tip-toeing and an unspoken bias that poets will be poets and boys, boys, especially in Bates' thrice asserted proposition that Ted was faithless to all his later lovers because of, wait for it ... 'his loyalty to Sylvia.' Do tell."[9]

Pretty fair minded demo job, huh? And why didn't I think of that – being disloyal in order not to be disloyal? To intentionally injure yourself not to have an accident. But I must be getting old; the whole Sylvia/ Ted/Assia reality show ("*Cheaters?*") is beginning to make me tired.[10] Dead, betrayed women and an annihilated child. Nothing the lads did, Ted, Wevill, Alvarez worth it, Sylvia another order of value, maybe worth it in a way, only she could make the valuation, her own life. I mean death. She very carefully spared her children if forgetting that coal gas, heavier than air, descends and so nearly asphyxiated her downstairs neighbor. Moral: in these matters (life, death and everything else) we can never be careful enough. Poets,

---

9   See Jonathan Bate *Ted Hughes, an unauthorized life*. The near equivalent being my being deliberately, methodically, one might say mechanically unfaithful because I could not bare the prospect of being so "accidentally". At least I didn't write any *grubby* poems about it and neither, to his credit, did David *Wevill*.

10 So old, that I recall vividly the time when a new book by a minor-major poet (Merwin, Justice, Nemerov, et al.) was not only anticipated and sought after but acquired, an event conceptually if not chronologically coeval with my seeing the last living Confederate veteran, in 1957. [Possibly John Salling (1856?-1959). It is now known that all such "last veteran" claimants after 1955 were impostors. – ed.]

real ones, usually are hazardous to your health. [None of it, the entire nexus, even including *Ariel*, worth the death of one (as it happened, Jewish) child, little Shura.] [3]

After the glide of dreams, grit.
Why are the squirrels shrieking?

5. Nov. 28   I used to pray to sleep well (and I seldom did) to have energy to face the day; now I hope to expend myself in the day to sleep well to have deep dreams, a reversal of priority. Such is my life, not yet over and I resist, I hope, the litany of age related physical problems of interest to no one, except clinicians whose work it is and not always them. A miracle to have reached with no significant medical problems an age at least 90% of humanity never reached, including the very great, Bach (did, just), Beethoven, Shakespeare, never mind the doomed geniuses, Marlowe, Purcell, Chopin, Mozart, Schubert, Mendelssohn, Schumann, and all the ones we never even knew to mourn. After age, pick one – sixty seems good to me, it's all bonus anyway; surely you have lived as long as is needed to mate, to parent, to become yourself and contribute to the human hive. Why are people so seemingly contented to be a debilitated liability, well, they have gotten into the habit of living, are afraid and see or have no easy means to exit. To think that most of my life was wasted in folly (not always bad, mind you), foolishness and lack of focus. Delete those years from time and my productive meaningful life ended at, say, age twenty-eight. Call me Keats.

I'm reminded too of the "Chinaman Proposition" and how it used to morally outrage me. If you were to be granted ten years of added life past your normal death point or a night with the woman of your desires if you were to press a button that would kill an unknown "Chinaman", would you do it? I thought, no person would do that. Now I think, what if the deal were that you could again feel physically like you were when you were thirty? I begin to equivocate. Maybe it is a sad Chinaman, a poor man who can't stand his life, a bad Chinaman, a disagreeable, age racked ugly one – surely it wouldn't be that bad – knowing what I now know of humanity, our daily malfeasances, to press that button? (He's gonna die anyway and is one less burden on mama Gaia.)

Another bright November day, warming in the sun, slightly shivering cool in the shade, one traverses latitudes in a few inches. The cat is pleased, tail up, stepping high, confidently patrolling her property. [30]

Pivot at twilight –
the hummingbirds no longer hover;
fireflies, flickering, begin to rise.

6. Dec.1 Aphorisms rise up (something I'm not bad at, see my …) but on a day when the mist thickens in the trees and glossy crows strut the grounds, I deny them. I've had it, frankly, with aphorisms a*phoristically* diminishing the True. What aphorism could encapsulate or express, say, my working life, the utter futility of it, in forty years of a forty hour work week, the stark realization: I never helped a person in a way that mattered, never improved the world, never did anything but earn a living (and what was that but acquiescence in the ultimate regime of social control) and most futile, those fervent youthful investments, totally intense expenditures – my work on library exhibitions, every item placed for display with surgical precision, my ten hours a week broadcasting, preparing to broadcast chamber music, rehearsing every to-be-uttered phrase as if resonance could convert even one person to beauty – let's face it, it meant nothing, touched no one, made nothing better but even worse, the realization that I confused being good humored with being good. As to aphorisms, what to say: they satisfy yet don't fulfill, the snack (smack) of truth. Or vice versa.

Which leaves us with writing: diagramed along two manifest axis – the narrative the story what happens – the horizonal, and the vertical, characters defined, refined and deepening. Truth to tell, writers mostly posit stock types of characters – the good guy, the bad, the fleckless lady, the girlish victim, the sage, and then propel them through a story. Even Tolstoy does this. Others are more developmental but the conclusion still holds in the exchange. A diary such as this short circuits the apparent development of character since the enunciating author is on stage even as the supplied protagonist relates his day, expositing along a seeming single line. What matters, the words that embody the otherwise ineffable thought. Since truly the only significant thing about our lives is the perpetuation of pure physicality passed and revitalized via variation, the DNA via children, (love generally) and what most identities us – our typical cast of thought, best preserved in words.[11] From Time's perspective what matters least is generality what matters most to us, the broad swarth of

---

11 Oh, yeah "and culture." Mustn't forget culture.

normal actions and specific thoughts where we live our daily lives. Encapsulated in words, the words are vivified as read to have life in your mind like actors on a stage. Which, as you well might have wondered, is the point of this, these marks you read, my tracks through life. I live repletely as you scan them. Granted, it is mostly pretty disagreeable, something about the umbrageous tone, not nice and there you have it. [But I've been nice my entire life, nobody more courteous, considerate, generous, modest and if you say "Whoa!" – nobody like that could write that – think again. It is you who are hubristic in the matter of your presumption; you have NO idea what it's like.] If I had my liberty, I'd snarl.[12] As it is, I am what I am, a kind of blue jay that sqawks, charls, a claw scratch on life's dome of multi-colored glass. A run of words, Pepys' diary? The 20th century Boston semi recluse guy what's his name John Turbot Brown (?) not right,[13] the much more interesting Lucy Pratt and include me in, The Harvard edition due me, after all, I gave them the third best years of my life, should have at least as many pages of notes, index, introduction and general apparatus (whatever that is) as originating text. [*Page, listen to me. Nobody cares, could or should. Got that?*] Roger. But still they tilt the great dish of the radio telescope to broadcast twenty seconds of Bach's little fugue (orchestrated!) to some staticy quadrant of the plasmic cosmos and nobody, absolutely nobody is listening. It is done as an expression of identify, okay, "This we were." We don't care that nobody cares. Which raises the old question first

---

12 *See Much Ado About Nothing*, 1.3

13 Arthur Crew Inman (1895-1963), "mediocre poet and voluminous diary writer", a lengthy selection of whose jottings was published by Harvard University Press.

asked by, I forget. Would we, humanity, choose to do it all over again? Without variation, an exact repetition. Given the ratio of meaning and futility, of beauty and pain?[14] And a little too much Famous Grouse.[15] [16]

0. Sept./Oct. [*The following entry is undated and is placed at random, without chronological indexing – ed.*] If I am walking down the street and stopped by an old man. who says "Timon is having an interesting day. He awoke and the canaries were free. Later, his horse took the high ha-ha for the first time. Tonight he expects call from his publisher" my first response, even before "Why are you telling me this?" will probably be to ask "Who is Timon?" He has four possible responses: Timon is a friend, someone he knows; Timon is a character in a story; he is Timon or no reply. My expectations, engagements and satisfactions radically differ depending on his answer. This is the nutshell that I am turning over, squirreling with in *Laminations*.

---

14 In a sense a trick question since one can never be sure the life you are leading isn't a repeat so that to answer "'no" is to advocate one's annihilation. This is the kind of facility that got me B+ or A- on student philosophy papers; not good enough in the tight professorial market of the late 1970's to justify proceeding to grad school.

15 I have spent many hours, working on it like a koan, wondering what could make a grouse famous. Perhaps it is a secret of the Illuminutti. I hoped it was because one got away, if not to tell the tale, at least to roost in the annals of branding. Maybe it was merely meta ; a grouse was put on a whiskey label, enough, surely, to fable any bird. Or posit a first vat of the yet to be enfamoused hooch, called "Grouse."(I mean, you wouldn't call it "Wild Turkey", would you? I should look it up. But I prefer being deep in my second Grouse on a winter day when, the twilight being short and intense, I come close to an answer, hearing the whistle of dove's wings before (seeing) the pulse of living flight.

Now, even at noon, it is obvious the light is aslant; every object is slightly chiseled, seen in relief, the famous crispness of fall due to angularity as much as the clarified lens of air.

7. Sept. 30 Having demonstrated my strong dispositions, time for some manly opinions.

I don't believe most of the balderdash about literature; literature is mostly tracks, a position perhaps too well tailored, for this daily tract. If it seems really important to you ... for various reasons, you do it, you "do" literature in the same way you do train spotting, or bird watching, fine. But in itself it is no more important than, say, veterinary science, electrical engineering, chess or plumbing. Less important than plumbing (the day will come when you will desperate for a plumber, a leading man, and no like day for a poet) – and sports a lot more pretension.

Unless, I repeat, it matters to you in the near crazy way anything may matter to anyone.[16] Or linguistic philosophy: "objects only exist in language." Er, tell that to my cat, wanting her ball. "Oh, what I meant was objects "as objects" only exist in language", which simply means, language has meaning in language. [Would you say Wittgenstein is overrated? Yes, Wittgenstein would be the first to say so.] Golly, who knew? "We" are getting

---

16 It must be said that the status of everyday language among humans is typically overrated. What makes us human are the grand or extended narratives of science, history and myth, the greatest of these being literature which is not only a carrier of knowledge but a form, one of which is contradiction. It was Henry James who killed me as a fiction writer since after first reading (1977) his late works, I thought "everything else is trivial." Except Shakespeare. That is still (2016) the case.

"nowhere" "here". Yet whole philosophical careers have been built on less, which is to say more.[17]

Shelving in the library, I passed a small assortment of Tom Swift titles, books that I devoured when I was 10-12; *Tom Swift and his flying submarine, Tom Swift and his atomic earth digger, Tom Swift and his supersonic monorail, Tom Swift and his perpetual motion prick*, when what I was really waiting for (only seventy years too soon!) was a Tom Swift brand electric female fuck bot.[18] Now you might think the additional of "electric" superfluous but Victor Appleton the third wasn't master of adjectives and a pseudonymous Yale man for nothing. Only very rarely have I wished my name was Chip and had gone to Choate, Yale, and wedded, headed to partnership, Patricia Fulsome Melon, she of the hefted hair, whipcord pants and trust-funded dressage.[19] Instead, I wed, very deliberatively, when I needn't have and "knew better", no securities, no trusts, BF. In fact, I knew better than to let her slip. After all, she was very valuable; she could never again betray me. Priceless immunity, I wasn't going through that again. At worst it would be as it had already been, an interesting ride. She has many fine characteristics (aside from those with unambiguous erotic aspects, nothing one should boast of, I agree, these virtues

---

17 My personal philosophy has always been "Sir, I am a true labourer: I earn that I eat, get that I wear; owe no man hate, envy no man's happiness; glad of other men's good, content with my harm; and the greatest of my pride is to see my ewes graze and my lambs suck." AYLI, III,2,1186-1189.

18 *Consumer Reports* gives the Yamaha Geisha Six its top rating, but there is a waiting list (2016).

19 Second cousin to Jodhpur Dabney Patton, nephew of the famous general whom some say was a cross-dresser.

are common; just see how the world is peopled). The obese, benign in his desk duty mode, county sheriff was touched, yeah touched by our doing the right thing, being present, vaguely guilty, before him, his piglet blue eyes bright with tempered tears, his lower lip quivering as he reached for the laminated card that inscribed the official state vows and asked ... "How long you folks been together?" We had the long faces of the long togethered. "Nine years. We've been eating the apple nine years". And so he rose, turning the laminated card over to read us, in his pastoral Virginia accent "the long form" that augmented the official words with an (self-composed?) account of how Adam and Eve were the first married and how the animals, deer, squirrels, rabbits, some ten named, had gathered around to shyly witness the foundational union.[20] At the end, his welcome to redemption grin, made glorious by two gold capped teeth. It was all as sweet as could be except for the fat black revolver slapping on his hip, (this the still innocent age when cops had not yet up-gunned to quick trigger, thirteen shot Glocks.) Speaking of weapons – and a man hankers after weapons his entire life – It is going to be very pathetic, all those burning-sinking American aircraft carriers and would be even more if they had been given emotion evoking ship names rather than those of moribund jarhead presidents-the Bush, the Eisenhower, the Ron Old Reagan (drifts about), the Carl Venison, dear me, a staggering maritime malapropos. At least the Sino-American War will be brief and not too destructive – not the first one. (It is

---

20 Presumptively, a pre-lapsarian event, humans and beasts being equally innocent, everybody friends. Later the animals would be hunted, herded, harnessed just as I have hitched my complaints and over-worked them for all they were worth. As to BF, it must be said "Wheresoever she was, there was *Eden*."

always the second in the series that's really intense, folks get focused, the Punic, the Anglo-Dutch, the Argentine-Paraguayan, the European world wars).

Reading: Bataille – unrelenting mediocrity; that I bother to try him, for the sixth time, indicates my own mediocrity. There has never been a good librarian intellectual. Why? They have read too much to take their own fancies (and never had the genius to make them seriously to begin with and so read a lot) seriously enough to achieve them at the usual "great" rate of simply "over do it". A great deal of quality, perceiving and possessing it, resides in the quick apprehension and rejection of junk. (80% of everything is junk, this no exception.) A great deal but not all of what is taken to be great is simple over-the-top-ness. Real greatness happens naturally and is almost simple. Or so they say.

The grand delusion of my most brilliant friend that Deleuze's would be the philosophy of the 21st century, risible in retrospect (when it's already a helix of computer and brain science, call that deleuzian if you want to). And who was Prof. Twit to say my poems were crude? When his dissertation was on the verbally ham-handed saw bones Dr Carl Loser Williams? Or that well groomed dissertation getter, bow-tied and glib, who sneered ("Your kind of poetry personally offends me", words emanating from a presumed friendly quarter where I'd positioned no defense) in his pruned, plumy vox, whose scholarly book on a cooked-up topic, "poetic mediations", published by an admittedly very sound second rate academic press, no one has read these thirty years (I checked our library copy's date due slip to make locally sure, his work gathering no habitation, no name.) Like everyone, I have scores to settle but honestly, only three or four. Okay professor, how else should you be offended, other than personally?

My first wife, the crazy one whom myself being young male mad only made her more so, she who made BF seem more or less normal which was, maybe, a life plan, used to quote mechanically (as my mother did her favorite nursery rhymes) a medieval saying that she got from what – the Ancient Rule or Piers Ploughlunch I forget – "Ever the longer the less the more."[21] Now I understand it – ever the longer to live, the less of a life, the more welcome death. Which will be my only comment on death.[22] Must reread

---

21 She was one of those people if heard convulsing in another room, it was impossible to determine, on the basis of prior behavior or immediate context, if she was laughing or crying. To quote a poem from that era (1975): *Liberated and learned/my husband washes dishes/to the "Emperor Concerto", /sleeves rolled,/he whistles like a piano –/grand at parties,/talking all he knows/about his heroes/ Beethoven, Michelangelo/for five minutes/a crane fishing in the shallows,/I kiss his feet, I lick his lips./He admires my brain,/calls me his lit'l Liebe-nitz./Nights, he stalks my calculus/smiling incontinence and impotence,/Oh narrow hipped lean spearer/I am your bathysphere.* ("Cranium") Not too bad a poem for a 23 year old, replicating Lowell and Plath's confined mania, one degree chilled, the best thing, its unsparing self-portrait. I carefully typed five copies on Crane's Best (100% acid-free cloth bond) and gave the initialed (not pretentiously signed) sheets to my then best friends; Karen, Joel, Bill, Sol and Judy. Does even one of those sheets still exist – in a drawer, a box, a file, folded in a book? I doubt it; all recycled, trashed, used to start the fireplace. I've ulcerated about the papers more than the pals, frankly. What became of them? Easy to find them online only my desire to is not as strong as my desire not to, Which isn't quite true either; every friend lost is an enduring diminishment.

22 The contemplation of one's individual death is a sad, lonely business. Apocalypse, on the other hand is a communal affair, with

Emily D. on death, no one better. Also excellent on bees. Also squirrels. Which is to say, life. [24]

Tinted scent of the poppy; whose kiss was that?

8. Sept. 10   Virginia suggests: "write about ageing as a new birth." Did she? When it is, passing a certain midlife meridian, a lessening, a daily diminishment even as it enables the decaying luminescence of greater clarity and notional stability (there being a lot less bubble in the stew) A losing war on all fronts. An old man on an old horse, "Donne-in" you might say.[23] Yet my project is to make a daily record of the campaign, a battle diary – an object of conceivable interest (what patterns are emergent?) if a lot less and a lot less brilliant than Virginia's, with all that metaphorical flash and fecundity – the woman was whacked, brain flares, hyper-yak. Text book manic/depressive. An alcohol/ nicotine addict, why don't her admirers just say so! Or as they, (Tom Crewe, *LRB* 31/3/16) do say more politely "She possessed a conversational brilliance liable to be iced with cruelty, an intensity threatening always to pitch into dangerous hilarity." [Not very nice [of me], you think? Please understand that "not very nice" is one of the few ways writers have of making a music-like transition from major to a minor? Odd how a painter can depict any old horror from that pit of thematic depravity, mythology, and not be smeared with a broad-brushed charge of negativity.] Granted, Virginia sees on average

---

lots of camaraderie and few, if any, survivors to envy. This is why more and more folks, as indicated by artifacts of popular culture, are avid, if unconscious, fans of mass annihilation.

23   See Donne's *"Riding Westwards"*.

fifteen people a week (every week) – lunches, teas, dinners, parties, meetings, Clive, Hugh, Lytton, Nessa, Mary, Ethel, John, Maynard, Saxon, Duncan – to name a few of them, bright squawking birds in a topical rain forest of intellectual fecundity. Who do I see? Once a week, briefly R and once a month G and 24 hours a day, BF. R & G – Rosencrantz and Guildenstern? God, Hamlet is a heartless ass – R&G dead, no prob (they deserve their own play) Ophelia dead, and sure he does get upset on an sheer ego basis ("I loved her more than ten thousand brothers so let's mud wrestle in her grave.") Polonius dead, no prob, (one more notched victim for our slippery princely sardine), the good old guy who knows it all, plays dumb and is trying to save everybody, a moderate "man for all seasons" much more justly than "Burn more protestants" More. Yeah, deserves HIS own play.[24]

As to BF, her cipher stands for "Break Faith" – she who always has her moments of stimulation, even brilliance.[25]

---

24 More aptly, *A Man for All Seasonings*, who curries favor with the king, bears his mace, peppers everyone with advice, minces with the queen, rues Ophelia's relationship with Hamlet, is assaulted … ("Enough spice jokes."- ed.) The play begins with a spotlight on the unopened curtain. Some vintage British actor totters out. "You all know the standard story. Now here's what really happened." It is going to be a long night. Alternatively, *Hamlet, the* (hip-hop?) Musical. My only request of the bright Broadway type who develops the idea is that he/she donate one percent of the profits to PETA. As to Polonius, he has become a father figure/mentor to me, his famous sage words might have been the epigram of this book – "To thine own self be true, write as thou wouldst read and thou canst not then be false to any art."

25 To those who think it might be ungracious to make the identification or extend the epithet, it should be noted that she affirmed this characterization over many months, with no concern about who

33

Well, she would, wouldn't she? Grant that and I do.

Indeed, she has many outstanding qualities, some, surely, that surely aren't the reflected display of my besotted projections.[26]

For much of my life, I thought she was a goddess (and before meeting her, conceived, actually visualized a deity that was she, tall, stern, dark haired, cruel) – all the divine archetypes, Athena, Venus, Artemus, Hera. (A piece of writing from the 1965 hack-historical novel *Clodia*,

---

knew, excepting one person, her victim, yours truly, so that it would be at least ironic for me to be the to preserver of purdah and careful curator of reputation or withholder of her functional identity, As to the imagined Edwardian gentleman, tapping me concernedly on the shoulder with his golden goat head cane, saying "Be mute for yourself, old chap", I say, when everyone knew, there is only risibility in being the last person to cozen ignorance.

26 Her actual appearance, a pale faced Nefertiti in casual Friday mode; speaks and reads French, German, Italian, reads (fluently) Latin and ancient Greek, peruses with understanding, Old Norse, Russian and Spanish, conversant with every significant work of literature; 'Hamlet's sense of time, the ethics of lying in Sophocles, Dickens's names for cats, weaponology in Icelandic sagas" among recent topics of domestic discussion; plays piano and harpsichord okay, musters an adequate game of chess, can walk five miles in peak Virginia heat without working up a complaint or sweat, other physical attributes as aforesaid, negative qualities, passim. Moves like a dancer, lies like a cat. [Of course, the adumbration of a lover's attractive attributes is the most overt type of self-compliment even if in this case where I aver my utterly average abilities as a foot soldier in life's army except for a quality of devotion, laser like in its focus and intensity if again of no mentionable merit since she hit all my switches. Paradoxically compounded of both irresistible force and immovable object, it has the power of always flat-footing the feckless, the unfaithful, the uncommitted who perforce must resist or adhere.

"She was tall, graceful, with dark piercing eyes and black hair, with a curious knowing smile as if she were about to pounce on me or cut open my heart and recite the contents, combining the beautiful and dangerous, like a knife, like leopard, like a thorny rose." fits my image of her perfectly, suggesting we are dealing not with a real individual as described but a not uncommon fantasized object of desire.) Oh, no doubt, she, women generally are better than men, no doubt but the man who idealizes anyone is headed for a fall. Practically speaking, from the woman's (Eve's) improving point of view, the chap needs education if not the slap of downright correction. You know, for his own good and the advancement of humanity. Now eat this apple. It's a wisesap. But what – you want to know – was Donne's horse's name? *Idunno*. Greek, I guess, for "Trotter" which, if you think about it, is one helluva of a gig. [21]

First snow, no one knows if the fox is sleeping or watching.

9. Oct.10   Two weeks since my last entry. So okay, we took the train (let it be recorded, on time both directions) to see the Wtewael exhibition at the National Gallery. His stylistic mannerist human forms, exquisite, unearthly colors, his technical mastery, especially in the small self-illuminating paintings of partying gods on copper sheets, sexy stuff but emotionally meaningless, shallow, smart sassy art by a chap who, successful artist and rich merchant with lovely wife and kids, looks businessman smug. To think that there was a time when this was my ideal of art – slick smoothness, my ideal too of love until I had it and after, knew better.

Hegel was wrong (But Hegel's system will accommodate its own error, the test of any philosophy).[27] The conceptual, aside from being in some sense analyzable – is always false, which sounds like that utterly third rate thinker, Bataille. The Buddha, who as received, is at least as real as Jesus, that is, not very – is right, the true is the empty, utterly unfalsifiable unity. But I expect Emptiness (which, oddly, you get at by utilizing a lot of non-emptiness – imaginary gods, chants, bead counting, incense burning and so forth) is not something that some of us, with immense meditative exertion are headed towards but a thing we are fleeing from. Take the Eden story: paradise is already behind us. We want(ed) it that way. Because non-conceptual "pure" being was boring, we had a appetite for thoughts, concepts as consumable things, illicit intellectual erotic objects we loved and hence the long invention of the passionate/painful world as lived, except by gurus, who resemble those redneck reclusives hunkered down on their ten acres in the back woods, at oneness, but at what cost, with nature. Alienation is our natural niche. You know, I liked me a lot better when I wasn't prone to these neat pronouncements. When I only owned questions. [4]

The winds were blows that blew themselves out.
A still morning, dew jewels on the rose.

---

27 We can perceive what he could not, that his system is a vastly intricate fragment, making his debates with Schlegel, the advocate of almost systematic fragmentation, ironic. Indeed it is Schlegel who conceived of "the irony of irony", which along with his "combinatory poetics" provided the theoretical argument for this book two hundred years before the author, post scriptum, knew of it. See *The Laboratory of Poetry,* by Michel Chaouli (2002)

10. Nov. 25   Yesterday, she was nearly killed crossing the street, at twilight, at the corner. In the zebra stripes, I was in the lead – a car some distant away, it wasn't dark we should have been readily visible, she oddly was slower behind me. I got across and unaccountably, the elderly driver had not only not slowed but had speeded up and I turned to see her still six feet in the road. I took her hand and pulled her forward just as the vehicle passed, an inch from her with a cold rush of air, I was stunned – she hadn't even seen it. That night the obvious mediation, the millions of beings that have lived and died, all the birds and cats and dogs from our childhood on, a massive bio-recycling, new birth and with every new birth a destined death. What can it mean? With large imaginations, we devise answers, religions and philosophies and myths. I suspect our lives amount to no more than an organization produced according to bio/physical processes that develops and then deteriorates, producing a temporary point of perspective, the person, no more than that. Yet to conclude that is also a categorical matter of imagination, that a concession that maybe something rather than nothing lies on the other side of our admittedly limited imaginations and cognitive boundaries, a hope. We should not be too sure.

The leaves finally all fallen (personal German for "completion, "Die Allfallen") and swept, over 36 plastic bags full, not counting the reefs made by pushing then to the streets. Rank on rank, they shine in the sun like *Cuirassiers*, headless and horseless but ready, arrayed for battle. [2]

Though the cat sleeps, it sees with killer's eyes.

11. Sept. 17   All the hummers flown except one, what is she thinking in her tiny, vivacious brain?[28] Me, I'm cutting down from three glasses of wine to one and half with god know what ill-effect. Last time, after four days of effortless abstention, I spent two days in delirium (no visions, just misery) in bed, unable to move. They call it AWS, alcoholic withdrawal syndrome. Am I an alcoholic-mentally, no, since I had no craving, never imbibing before 5 PM, but a matter of physical habituation, unthinking and yet the wisdom of it, free-will submission to a chemical, an act of radical free will that isn't free. Drunks are the ultimate ironists.

Wrote the *London Review of Books* concerning reviewer's account, her two mistakes in review of the new Wollstonecraft biography (since I was co-incidentally reading Todd's op cit.) They don't like me, never print my print letters on prissy points of correction [then three weeks later they did, a minor item about, of all people, Tennyson about whom I know almost nothing, except the point made.] so let's see how they like these American apples (they liked me enuf to respond, saying they were sending my letter to the reviewer – sure to be charmed by my tough Marovian (Philip, not Chris) manner, tendering no reply) – Wisesap. All in all, I'd say this is about as interesting as Alan Bennett's published latter day diary

---

28   The Aztecs, as crazy a people as can be conceived, as madcap as Romans, properly worshipped a hummingbird as chief god, which didn't prevent their killing thousands of the actual birds for their feathers. Still, the Aztec word is evocative, "ztinztum." Filling the feeder, one hears an insistent buzzing and turns to see a fierce, cross looking microscopic bird face, two black pins' head eyes stuck in bright green enamel, pointing its tiny saber beak at you. "Move."

excerpts (a man too tamed by time) only without, I'd guess the meaningful presumption of the associated work. But who cares about that, really? I give myself credit for skipping the uneven steps (staircase, rather) of the works. Who needs 'em – ever step into a large library? I gather most writers don't. They should, I do, every day. Or shouldn't if they tender pretensions of their worth.

Hence no doubt my method – and my malaise. To be an ant carrying grain to the literary storehouse? I'd rather chirp with the grasshoppers.[29]

Of course, I'm very grateful to BF. Only child of a widowed mother,[30] I was the center of mama's universe, and she of mine. I grew up self-absorbed, and despite the rough and tumble of the public schools, trusting, hopeful, selfish, short-sighted, in a word, spoiled. BF's revelations – polite term (the devil was the details; see my *A Book of Emblems* for one version of the true story) blasted my every frame of reference. For the first time I experienced real pain (and after thirty years accommodating that pain, the pain re-sets grows again ingrown, self-poisoning and narcissistic). Poor me. Whine. (As Auden observes, the poet must be shocked out of his "ivory tower" of complacency and self-conceit. The pain must be real, abiding, with the narrowest path of renewal and authentic engagement spanning deep gaps of self-pity and bitterness.) So yeah, thank you, BF. To be

---

29 In the words of the admirable James Merrill, in literature, "We have gone from the unspeakable to the unreadable." By which he means the non-readable, stuff you might read but really, why bother, a universal background radiation of null words. What about transcript or testimony? True crime. Any takers?

30 A traditional recognition phrase among Masons.

fair, after being bad, she was good.[31] Me, I was asleep in the dream of ego. And then I woke. Wrong to say, crudely, Identify or the Self isn't real, wrong to say it is. Identity is "in between", liminal.

Today's an evening entry, the day dead behind. We walked a mile and a half downtown and back, as every Friday, to the wine shop. We drink too much – it isn't healthy over 24 weekly "units" – as if time itself is salubrious. "Doc, does it matter? "Well, yes if you want to a stay well." "Yes, but does it matter?" Let me say, I have no interest in fiction, writing it or reading it. Our lives are fictive enough, fictive as history.

No, they aren't. I ache, therefore I am. No character is in pain.[32] And don't forget the existential reflux; it's the walking to buy booze that keeps us alive. [20]

Your brightest smiles were lies. Not, for that, to be extinguished.

---

31 Of course, all narratives of this type are philosophically naïve, being based on such dubious notions as self-access to inner states, free moral choice and responsible selves. Yet those who should know better, cognitive scientists, philosophers of mind and non-ego Buddhists behave no differently than everyday folks. The illusions have a natural and dramatic credibility. Why is that?

32 The point of *Laminations* being (and easy to perform a negative) not to resolve itself into the unity of fiction, characters that explicate and are explicated in characteristic actions, framed by notions of nature and society, themselves characterizations. It is not to deny the magnificent effects have not been achieved by masters of the novel but to assert that the successes ossify into readily replicated normative literary gestures that are boring, understandably inciting radically reactionary responses that at best (Beckett) are self-negating. Not that my saying makes it so or that you ought to agree with me and I hope you don't.

12. Nov. 16   The leaves now mostly all fallen, a major natural project one should not rake for granted. Doing the last rakes, chatting with Sarah, my 93-year-old neighbor, she told me how as a child in 1920s, she went to the laughing highland spring for all the family water and drank it unboiled. How the spring fed a small stream that had a shed over it. In lidded brown ceramic jars the family stored in the cool water, their butter, milk and farm cheeses, how her sister discovered she could skim a small cod of clabber, hold it in her cupped hand under the clear flow and a tiny trout would come up regularly to eat, tickling her submerged palm, her pet until the little girl grew up and the fish, in natural time both, died. Now the leaves trees are mostly bare and in the early morning the trunks catch the rising light, look like gilded boles, an amalgam of copper in the gold, the rosy tint, heavily laid on. But the ginkgos, mustard yellow, are still flush as burning swords and will stay so until, a week from now, the leaves will all drop in a single day to make an erotic spotlight for the lissome unsheathed tree. [13]

Coldest night of the year – the poppy seed splits;
First heat of spring.

13. Nov. 18   At this time of late autumnal warmth, (formerly called Indian summer-implying ricks of grain, stacks of hay, golden meadows, a quiet moccasined native on leaf paved tracks, Dvorak) a lovely masquerade happens after a day of light, silent rain, on the next day's sun, vapors and odors rise, an earthy, fertile smell that intuition identifies as spring, life coming on in March even as one knows it is mid November, a pleasing mental double take.

Reading the *TLS*, a review of recently translated novels by the Argentinean exile author Juan Saer. English reviewer doesn't much care for them: "the characters are unrealized flat and unconvincing, they speak in philosophical (unrealistic) dialogues, there's no plot to speak of, the entire project at best, dull and pedantic." Zooks! My kind of book, my literary, or more exactly moraine, terrain. Because there is impoverishment of plenty in the overall hemispherical shape of things: hundreds of new, highly competently achieved fictions (plots, characters, actions) along with utterly grounded, researched non-fictional histories, studies and biographies – value in either well achieved but the total effect is of a too vast and un-innovative monoculture, there needs to be a new fusion or fraction: Iain Sinclair as a failed novelist or him as fantastical memorialist. Here, my intention, hardly in this personal fall an ambition, is recapitulated by my as yet candidate titles: *Days, Last Light, Fell Pyre, The Dark's Early Dawn, Going Through the (E)Motions* (too close to the bone, I think), *The Daily Weather, The Unburnt Diaries, Tracks* (as in footfalls, paths and musical segments, with a nod to the euphonious which is what I have tried to do in my prior books and am giving, in every sense, an attempt at here, what writers like Saer were doing too in some aspects so that it is a mistake and a limitation to see "tracts"), *"The Cunning to be Strange"* – a purpose, a ploy but also, as what is denominated, what's lacking ... "Madame, I use no cunning at all" ... what's so admirable about Juliet, her innocent and yet utterly sophisticated authenticity. If anyone were to read this, I'd like for them to skip around, touch the surfaces, go- stop- go like a water strider on a pond.[33] Roughly speaking, mine was the last

---

33 Journals/diaries can easily be classified as of three types: those

generation in the "first world" to reside in solitudes, a slick era of facile interconnectivity spreads like brilliant oil, one that will cure my complaint, if it is that and gentle critic it isn't, since people are losing already the singular focus, the fitness and follow through, the stamina needed to really read, to abide in their own and the author's solicitous solitude (because really why would anyone gyre around their mere ego when they could be online, sexting with Naomi or Ted) and, all neglect monuments of dated intellect.[34]

---

never intended for public exposure, those essentially written as private exercises yet with an eye to possible future publications (Woolf's, Powell's) and those, very numerous these days, designed at the get-go as books to be read, often recording some traversed trauma, *My Congo* or *Cancer Diary,* well written with wise saws and modern instances, the kind of serious volume taken up by adjunct professors, teachers, librarians, and middle managers of the more sensitive type – and forgotten a year later. My own effort differs from these at point of origin; my reading as a tender juvenile (age 11) such books as *War and Peace* and Kant's *Critique* that I could not possibly understand thereby defining the only worthy book a difficult one so that my ambition has always been to write something that was unreadable if not by virtue of its profundity then happily by dint of perplexity.

34 What has always bothered me about Yeats is that interwoven with the real beauties is a huckster type crassness; you either detect (or imagine) it or happily for your appreciation, you don't. To his credit, Yeats is forthright about the utility of "Lust" and "Rage" (his terms) as stimulants to creativity in the aged, a therapeutic "always already" lampoonable that needs to be subsequently succeeded by serenity and oblivion even if these scenics are naturally less engaging narratives. On the broader topic, if we leave the "reality" TV series *"Robot Wars"* out of it (an incredibly satisfying presentation of scientific advances, industrial design, tactics and mortal combat), the issues can be illustrated by comparing Shakespeare to any good 2016 TV drama series. The latter will be more accessible, more humane in lacking overt prejudice; its characterizations, if generally inferior to the Bard's, will always be adequate-good, its plots, in almost

Such clearances. This journal is transitional-unintentional, an upstart weed. Impervious to video! Another seedling title – "Weeds" – well everything is, transitional, that is. I like weeds. Indeed, my own facility and lack of focus and intentional ambition or even respect for genre is my filament of hope, that in transcribing my fluctious scope, it captures an outline of never devised form. Suddenly, I looked aslant and saw the right title.

That brings memories back, being in the Cambridge pub (still bosky if over-renovated with plastic knock-off (Taiwanese) Art Nouveau hanging lights, everything vaguely too bright though the smell – old smoke, yeast, fried fat and trace testosterone, old bloke, was indelibly legit) with the podgy Heaney hanger-on, just at that degree of fellowship (no closer nor distant) where he could say "How's your work?" I replied "Nobody is reading this crap, everybody is writing this crap." On ultrabright TV, the announcer went all girly-shrill over a missed goal, a player all Hecuba over a pretended foul. Talking only about my own work, this gross misappraisal was hurtful, wounding I mean to

---

every case, better. Shakespeare is consistently superior in only one thing – verbal realizations, (mostly) successfully transposable to dramatic effects. These have been vastly inventoried and justly praised but no one has explained, apart from lame pleas of "makes us human" and "a mirror to nature" why they matter or why they should continue to do so in 2116. But see my forthcoming book, *"A Shoal of Time."* To characterize such a discourse (this one) as "secondarily secondary" is correct, it being *commentary* of less than Empsonian or Auerbachian achievement, only in so far as one fails to see its function as marker in a foreground/background dynamic and as performative portraiture of a mind that's critical, naturally dialectical and fundamentally comedic. "Seriously".

Mister Podge who believed in the stuff generally and had hopes, oh, high reasonable hopes himself realized when the generous shamus of Heaney wrote him a recommendation to Princeton. Prince Professor Podge still has I bet that perennial looking for something hopeful squint framed by his Harry Potter glasses – a good thing in a didacter who should share (some) the inchoate and frankly immature outlook of his students, otherwise growing too grand and satisfied. The tenured professor; the tenderized boutique, be-spoken steak. Medium well-done, you might say. [14]

Grey wash on grey wash, the sky; a day before our meeting, a day before our meeting.

14. Nov. 22   I wake up just before dawn and wait for the birds to begin their great paean to the sun, and while less an event now than in spring/summer, there is still an orison this warm November. It sounds like an orchestra tuning up, the various avian punctuations[35] and is, excepting maybe, music and the voice of one's beloved, which are apprehended -appreciated in a differ registers, the most beautiful thing, in full vox, I have ever heard. The occurrences of which, given life in cities where the only birds heard are a few sparrows (chirps) or starlings (whistles) and the usual dearth of dead winter, is a lot less than my over 22,000 lived days. What have I learned in that time? That it is best to cultivate an attitude of compassion and generosity as the ground of all action. That a rational wariness is still useful because some people are malevolent or damaged and will do you injury. That in defense of this world's moderated goodness or of one's self, family, land,

---

35   !!*#@?;..,&::,#@!"';*#!..(+)*!@^^

culture and language, it may be necessary to inflict great injury on aggressors. That armies of Quakers and Buddhist mediators won't defeat Hitler (or, for that matter, Mao). That love and death are the great themes of life. That self realization in the deepest sense is not selfish but our essential existential labor. That there is immense significance to our apprehension-attachment to the world's beauty, only we cannot formulate an argument or thesis expressive of it. (Art, our best effort.) Reciting and mulling over these lessons can be done in a lot less time than the twenty minutes of the birds' cursive crescendo, a westwards heading rim of sound, during which my moral dicta begin to resonate like a smug credo and are immediately suspect. [22]

After the warmth of wine and laughter, the best thing was the coolness of the sheets.

15. Nov. 23   Lunch with G. I'd be remiss not to mention that he said my last book was "brilliant." I can't entirely credit him at either end, so to speak, that my work is or that he deeply felt it was. Friends are forthcoming with their natural flatteries. All "real" authors have lots of friends, which is why the quality of their work deteriorates so fast. Flattery being an erosive friction.

Reading Rilke, I was thinking, what would he make of the Paris massacre, yesterday, in his favorite city? Nothing I think because even though dying in 1927, his entire mentality is old order (pre-WWI) civility (and keep in mind, he had the gentlest of Great War experiences- an officer clerk, briefly in Vienna). Of all major poets, he is least able to encompass catastrophe, attuned to beauty, proportion, curvature, graciousness, the Victor Horta of verse, "Aber, er war", and almost Rilkeian line … but he existed, all that matters, *im besten Sinne des Wortes,* "woody", flexible, malleable, of various grains and finishes, I like the guy so much I'd love to trespass on his personal space, knock his knobby knee, touch his limpid hand,[36] a violation surely, but I am a nice guy, honest, modest too, in possession of my modest gifts, the most modest man I know and though you say "you could not say so even once and be so", allowances must be made for the trope and the joke of it. The scope.

First frost. No crickets sing.

16. Dec. 3 The climate control convention meeting in Paris, jaw boning over no enforceable standards, just "voluntary" posturing, China and India significantly underreporting their pollution for decades and surely in the future, in terms of going over the two degree Celsius average global temperature limit that mandates significant global warming, it hardly matters what North America, Japan and Europe do. In a sense the developing world is more culpable – try telling that to the enviro goody gooddies – because they, the third world leadership elites know the consequences as the originating polluters did not, not that they would have cared – think of all the carbon released in Europe's wars. The cost – incalculable human and animal suffering. Yet, beings are doomed to suffer. Art is going to suffer, specially that supreme (aside from

---

36 He was also the most attachive kind of moocher, if properly selective; his moochees could afford it and got in return exquisitely phrased, beautifully crafted calligraphic letters describing the month, say, they had just funded him at the best Swiss hotel.

language) human artifact, Venice, *La Serenissima* (for all its masculine swagger, most feminine of habitations) will not survive a two degree Celsius warming's melting icecaps, the rising seas and more forceful tides, no technology can save her. And while no one can intemperately adjudicate which damage is worst, the pain of creatures versus the destruction of Venice, it is a fact that art need not have been lost; it is from an arbitrary and wanton disregard of our highest value. Some of the art can be relocated, there will be photographs and in literature an epitaph, this most symbolic of cites (only rivaled by Jerusalem, and its symbolic-sacred order), among all the memoirs and studies, the greatest Ruskin's amazing, mimetic, if in miniature, of the place's beauty and complexity, *The Stones of Venice*. As to the inspiring place, I recall the poem of Sappho, "Some say, most beautiful – the abode of one's beloved; others, their hometown. I say it is Venice in her watery gown"; some translate the adjective as "shimmering", which adds a tawdry-tartist element not appertaining until her late, disgraced widowhood. Even then not so crass as a Venus di Mileage or a Colossus of Roads – I'm looking at you, Amerika. I'd choose a doge over a Ford, any day. No guarantee on a Cressida, that's for sure. (Enough traffic in car name punnage – ed.) [23]

The longer one lives, how strange to be here, now,
at this intersection of time and space.

17. Oct. 24   Reading *The German War* by Nicholas Stragardt, social history of WWII from the German side. Item: German colonel finds abandoned orphanage of Jewish children in Kiev, their parents already killed.

Appalled, he places a guard on the building to protect the kids from roving SS and Ukrainian nationalist killer gangs, radios the top army commander, urging that since they are children, they should be fed, turned over to the soviets or at least sent somewhere relatively safe. The order comes down. "Give them to the SS". I wondered why is pain in time processed as distance but in space as current? Granted, since we cannot spatially remove ourselves from our own pain, it is time that provides the remedy, if any. But isn't it all the same? These children killed and as a minor matter too, the likely sudden discomfort of the officer who must now see the sham and shame of his career – why don't we apprehend it as immediate pain? We have to make it right, right? Not well expressed, there is an issue here.

Yesterday had its light rain, the changing leaves so glisteningly bright from the cleaning they stood out like abstract colors on the limbs, I sat out until night fall reading a good book, *Branches on a Wire*. It was better than I remembered it. Better, surely, than the author had written it. [20]

At the end of my journey, sick.
Over the blasted, cold freighted fields
My dream lingers.

18. Dec.11.   Artists scuff the stuff of silence. Something hard prevents my forgiving her and this something also cut me off from the world. But the hard thing would speak. I too am real, part of the world, deny me and you are not yourself. The shame of it – to be deformed in such a conventional way, an event in biography. Just another item in the world's inventory of damages. The danger then: to be small, resentful, reactive rather than resilient, open, generous, one's life the breathing time of day 68 degrees and sunny no one can recall such a mild mid-December but the animals, the suburbs' invernal commonality – nuthatches, cardinals, crows, squirrels are happy. [18]

19. Dec.12   Aphorisms are untrue. That said, I'm very sympathetic to Sarah Manguso's, "I prefer writers' diaries to their work written intentionally for publication. It's as if I want the information without the obstacles of style or form." in *Ongoingness,* the rare contemporary book (2015) that engaged and pleased me. It's close enough to my own methods, hers a short book of aphorisms. Aphorisms are events along the vertical line of thought; by theme, her dicta are about her life passing, specifically, a meditation of her recordation of it in her voluminous diary, nowhere quoted, its existence for us (she herself says) a matter of faith. I think she doesn't get the full two dimensional localization, her thing is almost exclusivity aphoristic- with those strengths and limitations, simply referencing her daily diary doesn't lift her observations out into transactionality. I like – no matter the hits and misses of my execution – my idea better, a diary- normatively a narratizing and "historical" document, that presents apercus of thoughts as that day's mental events and so has meaning both "vertically" and "horizontally."

The issue is not so much one of scope and quality but of belatedness, of after-the- factness. Of being, personally, a mile wide and an inch deep. Fate.

Saw the film *A Dangerous Method*, about Jung, Freud and their gifted female patient, Speilrein. There are two, three scenes where S (played by Kiera Knightly) is bound to the bed's headboard and on her knees, stretched out, scantily clad spanked by the not quite young Jung to rip- roaring climax. Enjoyed these scenes so much (contrast to real pornography that's reliably boring) so much that in my excitement, I kept drinking, half a bottle of sparkling wine, two light beers and two inches of scotch. That's surely binge drinking, excess, though I woke the next morning feeling better than usual, no hint of hangover, indicating perhaps a dangerous tolerance or just a nailed landing on some sweet spot of glucose. The only symptom of my debauch, an odor of almonds (my drinks' accompaniment) and fine Islay hooch. An old man could smell worse. What does Emily D, one (Wollstonecraft, Weil, Townsend-Warner, Emila Bossana, some others) of my mystical brides, say (?) "That odd old man is dead a year, we miss his stated hat." "Stated" is brilliant. [35]

Eepitaph; the night jar's cry falling over fallow fields.

20. Nov. 1   Another day, nothing to say. I'm losing this war. Maybe it is time for a general survey of my any given day. The night before, I lie in bed, more alert than at anytime, drift off around 2, wake up at say 3, toss and turn, get up at 6 with the cat, pee, go back to bed really get up at 8:30, have a quick breakfast, some sweet bit and coffee, check the computer for local and national news, the weather and my email; defecate, take a shower, walk around the house; if the weather is good, do yard work, tuned to the season. Then out for the day's major walk and mission, grocers, wine, books, generally over two hours on foot; twice a week, volunteer work at the university library shelving, lunch at noon, then reading newspapers, magazines or more yard work or the cat's yard walk then always great heaviness. Around 2 PM, I go back to bed, read, nap, half asleep then up at 4 for another yard inspection, cat's dinner and my planning and cooking the human dinner – BF does cat's breakfast, litter box and wash-ups. Long lost, the ability to write poetry and as of last year, to even read it, the focus to listen to intense, complicated sounds – chamber music, the effort makes me tired and increasingly the inability to read anything for longer than half an hour, to have lost the capacity for verbal and sonic intensification, what's left? Well, I don't claim to have smelt or tasted enough. Not enough women,* desire endures and yes, there is still the crescendo of sex but frankly more a cruising at altitude, like checking a checklist than thrusting the throttle like it used to be. Yes, I have seen all I need, thought all I need, my brain is fatigued, the day is over at noon, we know where this is headed … and in truth I do begin to look forward to death as the next big thing, a something (as odd as life) or more likely, a nothing. Though since these are human categories, maybe there is a thing "in-between", a something nothing? Ok, this is about interesting as a 19th century classical music slow movement, a serious going through the motions, god what bore, why did anybody bother, especially my ingenious Mendelssohn? A tope day, grey light, no rains, warm leaves falling, the mole in its safe hole, the chipmunk in her habit.[37]

*(No, not enough despite that half year in England where, after the breakup with Frau Eins, I had gone to study

---

37 The clouds, like a reverse filter, adding matter, softening the light to make it visible to our earth bound eyes.

writing at the University of London, the incredible chance meeting with Major Writer, he not on the faculty, beaked and hollow eyed like a spate-spent trout, in the library stacks, our pints in the pub (The Gilt Edge), me a moon to his manhood minion.[38] Soon he was passing his junior division discards on to me (and probably his reviewers) – women who responded so enthusiastically the once or twice as if to ensure report got back to him what he was throwing away, their names that this dimmed in the past could be, in their reality, any name, Emma, Augusta, Carol, Beth ... all in all, ruinous – as "success" often is.[39] I returned to the States a year later just in time to meet, was this fated or what – BF. Mostly, the women were kind; I could write a book, "The Kindness of Women", (them) wanting only that demanding thing, to be loved. Easy to idealize them after, except now I know better.

As to Major Writer, he was a massive presence, with fullback body and Easter Island head, an authoritative northern voice smoothed by the Cam's silver tonguing. Oh, he *could* listen to you intently but mostly, he talked, slate blue eyes drilled into you, spellbindingly on things he knew, myth, poetry, writers, farming, fishing, publishing politics, taking up too much oxygen, moving in on your

---

38 Just prior to publication, my friend R., who knows a lot of law, informed me that in England a case of libel can be successfully prosecuted on the basis of "contextual prejudice", whatever that means, independently of the truth or falsity of the offending statement. Rather than a proper name, "Major Writer" must serve as a designation.

39 The "passing" mechanism as facile as (I enquired) as his earnestly asking his female friend to take a lonely young American admirer (of himself, Major Writer) out for a drink, *por favor*.

position, aggression to possess you, which if you were a woman might be compelling/captivating; if you were a man it was either resistance or surrender (I was Percival to his Yamashita). If anyone in the notoriously badger sett Major Writer's family objects to this depiction, well go ahead and sue; I'm blue watered incorporated in the Taulau Federation and good luck there. Through all the lean years, I sent The Taulau Sharks, the national rugby team, $1500 a year (on advice of my tax man since the team was a UN registered, US recognized charity, UNICEF with balls) to keep the lads in jerseys or at least Chinese jock straps.[40] Loyal people, they won't forget a friend. [29]

The oak splits in the storm; my enemy's hard face.

21. Sept. 12   In other words, odi et amo. A rather ovoid proposition.[41] Reminds me of my youth – electric sturm surges of energy venting into frustraious rage. Watt was the matter? Anything could set me off. Intensity tending towards murderous urges (not enough sex?) but hey, no one killed. Later, from early manhood, thirty plus years of even tempered conjugality with BF, a thirty years stretch of on average every other day aeorbic erotic exercise (Go ahead and criticize that phrase. Do you know what men are? It is all in Homer.) Averaging three times a week over thirty-five years – once a week even at Medicare

---

40   The team shirts – an attractive azure with silver shark profiles, are available from International Rugby Union (in Manchester) at Shop@RubyUnion.com for $40, plus $10 shipping. All shirts bear the name of Tippi Toppaumanoluo, the team's legendary offensive right wingman, whose goal in double overtime advanced the Sharks to the epic 2008 championship game against New Zealand.

41   Not Ovid but Catallus 85, "I love, I hate."

claimant age sixty-something, Doctor to geriatric patient: "Haven't you ____ed enough?" No wonder I could coin my beautifully crafted poetic phrase, one right up there with "still unravished bride of loveliness" or "bird thou never weren't."[42]—"three thousand plus fucks."[43] Note the dual adjectival application of "plus". Double plus is double plus, as Orwell used to say. Double plus in fact; fact and fate: fate = the sum of facts. All that gratuitous male force, anything to boast of? Aggression pumped into sex, a conduit. (see Rilke's *Hetaerae*) The Jizz Age. Nah, nothing to boast of. The world must be peopled. Thank "Great creating Nature". Now the juice is drying up. A squeezed lemon or leman. Again, in the words of my doctor "When a man is tired of sex, he is tired on life."[44] And guess what? As the juice dries up, like water seeping up in the basement, dark pools of returning rage. A matter of emotional hydraulics. I'm angry every day, over nothing, over everything, over age. Only I've a plan for mitigation, a conversion of rage, this diary, an entry a day. Three hundred plus funks. Exercise. Woolf without the wafty works. Sublimated anger. Did I say? Another lived day of lucid sky and sun. [33]

Autumn mists, the ache of memory.

22. Nov. 23   Went to see *Hamlet* last night at the local theatre feed from London, with the gifted young actor Cumberbund or whatever his name is, who was excellent

---

42   Keats. *Ode to a Grecian Yearn*.
43   From the author's "Autopornobiographies" in *Apex*.
44   Oblique reference to Doctor Johnson (1709-1794).

not that I endorse the play. The complex but fluent intellectual poetry is amazing, as is that lyrical tour de force about Ophelia taking a dip but as drama, once-and one viewing will do, once you get pass the mystery play who done it aspect (yeah, *The Mousetrap*) its not much good as drama because there is almost no emotional exposition or development among the principals; Claudius ever the most attractive figure in the play (despite young Hamlet's slanders, calling him a " a mildewed ear"), the internal proof being Gertrude's love; Hamlet a maladjusted, spoiled grad student, disturbed except when he isn't smart-assing-- to me only the brief scenes with Ophelia count as real drama., poetically brilliant but a dry gulch of exposition. If you don't see that *Hamlet* is Shakespeare's supreme drama of intellect (brain) and *Othello* his of affect (heart) – well, you don't see much do you? Because Shakespeare cares about Othello (and his situation) more than he does Hamlet, being closer to home. As close as a second handed bed.

We passed her, I hadn't seen for in thirty years but recognized her instantly and assuredly, Prof X, I recall the first time I saw her, 1984, in the bookstore, fall. Now, decades years later, I'm going to the theatre, she walking away from it and I thought, well if I do later see her at the theatre, it's an augury of true love and will write her- after all as a betrayed person, I am held to no standard morality, mine a largess earned/learned; her husband another professor, they had young married profs written all over them (we're cute, do adore us) and later learned who they were and what department, English natch. They were the golden couple of the era and granted she wasn't conventionally beautiful, a narrow face with small grey/green eyes but tall, smart wry, Angevin looking with a trace of timid/coy, what, sweetness, a fey graceful creature so yes, I recalled her and refreshed the image over that 30 years by infrequent look ups of her latterly online faculty portrait. And even before I left this one horse town 25 years ago, the story had broken and everyone knew it, Mr Prof – handsome, with a charming smile and aura of healthy male vanity, had left her for a comely Pakistani graduate student. Like all true crime, it happens somewhere everyday. So I knew her when I saw her yesterday, still narrow faced with age engraved guarded eyes- no fat or obvious sag, her lips firm, her glance at me looking at her direct and just that, what, sense of impact on her countenance, of her having been really knocked out of quilter, the long recovered from blow, being bashed/betrayed – it takes one to known one, a recognition. I saw it in her face. It's a subtle thing, not horrible, a look of resolution like you were driving and your car blindsided, turned around by the blow and damaged so you can't do a 180 turn and can only, being determined to proceed and live, drive in reverse, steering by an exacting focus in the rear view mirror… all those miles going forward, looking behind. It's an achievement, not one you wanted but it does distinguish, you are different, having the look for those that know. Not knowing my story, did she yet detect the shared experience in my look at her? Combat veterans. … yeah, the so called "long stare". Yo bro, I mean sis, been there.

She wasn't btw at the performance, love must wait, love loves to wait (and doesn't) to know itself. Wasn't there that poll back in 1968- would you prefer going to Vietnam or your wife betraying you and 50% preferred Vietnam although when they asked this of combat veterans, only 20% preferred combat which is still an amazing percentage unless that is the same portion of men that actually enjoy the horrors and hazards of war. Yes, betrayal in marriage is in the global marketplace of human misery, an adulterated penny, a pittance but in the scales of any human heart, it's the lowering lump of lead, for king and queen, man or mouse.[45] Can I fully forgive her for this hardening, for what is viler than having to calculate the amount of granted love? As if love was to be parried, like hard cheddar. [As in thrust and parry. To be threatened with a sharp cheese, a stiletto of stilton, is no laughing cow matter.] But then I think, she is soft, human, changing, expiring in the moment, a fragile thing at the edge (we all are) of death. In point of gratitude, she broke open my ego like an egg.[46] Not so hard boiled, after all. [10]

The sapling bending in the wind, something too about the young girl's walk.

---

45   As to mice, my two year battle with them for possession of the top floor of a 19th century Beacon Hill townhouse left me with high admiration for them as species capable of generating in very small biological packages, individuals of charm and courage. Like humans, in mass they are pushy, overpopulating, polluting and (as Kafka also records), loud. As to BF and Guy, I would not have allowed them a grain, an instant of human solace together, would send them to an eternity of Hell for even one enjoyed under conditions of breached trust, which I concede is so harsh as to be utterly self-damming, And for that, I really do condemn them.

46   I saw a long time ago that mine was a second rate mind, enlivened by a modest verbal talent and consistently undermined by distraction so that the miraculous moment of Zen like awakening would only arrive with the sound of one hand clapping, i.e., a slap in the face.

23. Dec. 4 I didn't record what meant much to me from three days ago, the misty morning. Walking aback from the library, I saw washed out and exposed on the sidewalk, a long (for this region) six inch rubbery earthworm, a catch for the still much in presence gross, gluttonous robins and so I stopped, found a twig and looping it on the stick, found a spot in a adjacent yard, first clearing off with my foot the mushy layer of leaves, and dropped it on the ground. The hard, clay soils need earthworms and I felt justified in my existence, at least for the day, that I saved such a valuable creature. I earned today's epithetic beauty (and immense karms of good karma), standing just briefly under the great campus ginkgo, a known historical tree, over 125 years old, still largely leafed but with views through the large reaching branches to the pure blue sky and I in the center of a immense golden circle of fallen leaves, a gold carpet, absolute beauty.

Reading Auden's *Dyer's Hand*, consistently impressed by his knowledge, soundness and humanity, I do disagree with his very period (1950s, gentlemen in grey suits, middle-brow culture, the murmur of Oxbridge common rooms) stricture that one should not air one's personal linen, the grubby personal stuff, in open literary light.[47] In my era, where all literary art is lowered, debased by deliberate facileness and crudity but also simply by the numbers of people who create it, embodying the truth that almost anybody can make art but only a few can make it good, there is a resource, a soundness in *the personal* no matter how grotty. Execution still matters, of course, but one is

---

47 As regards literature, Auden may be correct. But as for history, all of Clio's wardrobe needs a public airing, including her lingerie.

light years ahead by not having to expend effort to make somehow authentic the weakly conceived "artistic." Auden extols authenticity as the prime artistic value.

The news is out, the California shooters were a young Muslim married couple who left their baby with grandma. Why would the woman do that, killing innocents and knowing she is going to die? Is it the ultimate in wifely obedience "blow them away". "Yes, dear." Not quite the ultimate, which would surely be "blow away and blow job." The news cycle can accommodate one mass shooting a week after all this is capacious America but can it handle where we are headed, one a day? No, mass shootings will be relegated their own info niche, like the stock market or sports scores, Exxon 34.8, Ge 17.3, Chicago 7, Los Angeles, 14, data to be reported that will mean nothing to anyone except those personally invested, in this case, the living victims, their friends and family. Already nobody really cares. There is no debate. Mass murder has become a kind of reality TV. I am, btw, a proud gun owner. [describe, in lush, loving detail the weapon in question, the cozy fit of the warm wooded stock, the tang of oil and metal, balance of the aiming hand, the patina of history ...] because I know what men know: we love violence.

[34]

The wind rattles the dry twig of leaves. I should be far from here.

24. Sept. 31   Trying to read to conclusion, for the fifth time, *Failed Pire*. Thoughts, beautifully expressed ingeniously designed but so artificial, breath-taking in the worst way, a show-off baroque, so clearly the Nabob trying to out contrive Joyce – he has to be number one(being bald and supra-testosteronic) and of course dead rivals are best, they can't up their ante, Such ambition is self-subverting, the trying too hard. Beautiful sentences are not enough. The thing is airless with design, tedious in its gamesmanship (note: real games are better as games but just wait for VR), as dead as an ornithological drawer of stuffed songbirds. Structure to the point of suffocation, not to mention the sheer immitigable condescension of the entire project.[48] No surprise he would even condescend to Jane Austen in his published lectures, she who was blessed with a perfect pitch of written English. Now I doubt, as has been asserted, that Shakespeare "invented the human." If so, who invented him? But Aunt Jane surely, if not inventing, perfected a kind of supremely fluent "natural English." Made me reflect on mine its proclaimed simplicity, an honest diary, an account of the most basic lived unit, the day. Not ever to be read and if, in some quirk of infinite freedom, scanned, then skipped and scuppered.

Let me begin again. My honest chronicle, a daily recounting ... [I was asked to give a small talk, based on my work, to Antonin Kerschberg's 2106 Bowers Seminar. About my current project, I recall saying "After two or three days,

---

48 To be clear, I don't contest Nabokov's beauties only say they are spoiled for me by his mandarin condescension. Updike observes "His love of chess problems encouraged a taste for combinational complexity that can be mechanical and cumbersome. "Updike gets everybody's number. What's his? The best kind of narcissistic personality, with a high intelligence and imagination that is, perforce, outreaching and enabled by his boundless self-approval.

I read the last diary entry and feel no sympathy for the author or his sentiments, even if they are repeated in the next entry. It's nothing like the facilitating, ever retrievable forms of literary art, where, for instance, we experience Pierre Bazukhov as real even in his briefly sketched-out "I want a motorcycle or revolution" middle age. I feel only alienation towards my jottings and that, curiously, gives them objectivity and authenticity. I don't *personally* believe them – they must be true." Most of the kids were willing to play the game even though they much preferred author as aura to actual human being.[49] One asked "So what you're doing is fiction?" I said "It's the most intimate kind of realism – true and not true, the stories we tell ourselves about ourselves." This, which in the slightly strutting didactic tones of the classroom sounded okay, looks pretty lame written down. As to the kids, after forty-five minutes of my gyring self-involvement (following a brisk ten minute introduction by Prof. Kerschberg that touched on Herbert, Defoe, Richardson, Chamfort, Nietzsche, Wilde, Kafka and a brace of contemporary aphorists, Don Paterson and James Richardson) I hope they (the kids) had a nice evening of blogging, bonking, tweeting, twerping, reading graphic novels or whatever they do for enjoyment and self-revelation.] ... Yesterday, I dug with the small now rusted trowel, ten small holes for the tulip bulbs, life bombs, mines. Before dibbing in the bulb, I put a layer of the potting soil that was wasted in the small plastic pots

---

49 My general experience of such events is that excepting rare instances of real interest, evidenced either by monosyllabic enquires ("what?", "why?") or by complex constructions trying to capture the interlocutor's consuming curiosity (which they are almost afraid to reveal), young males question as self-assertion, females as self-seeking.

where for two weeks I had waited for the cat-grass seed to sprout. The seeds were dead. So, a hopeful investment in the next spring; how I love the sleeping potential of those bulbs, napping all the way from the Nether-lands, to stretch their sun awakening limbs in a bed of red Albemarle clay.

Yesterday too, we lost the dear little interloping tortoise shell cat who had claimed our yard and us as alternate owners. Her new home two houses over, after a month had proven untenable because of the resident dog and so the new owner called the old one, who rapturously reclaimed her, vowing never to give her up again (something in their new housing arrangements, finally resolved pro-cat), he confessing his grief at given her up and she, after a chase, asleep like a baby in his arms. Since we could not adopt her because of Storri, this was by far the best outcome even as we feel her loss. [Then just six months later, Storri dead, the complex organization that was her life, broken and she a dead soft weight, laid down in that same cold bed of clay. I lost my unthinking, moment to moment, confidence in life then. That much closer, then, to the end.]

Is this of any interest? No matter, I presume no reader. Which does not make it narcissism; the object is an analytic understanding of self, not its reinforcement.[50] For bone-fided narcissism, see any writer who assumes his made-up farragoes, a lifetime of them, are deserving and indubitably destined

---

50 Rather, it makes it optimistic; everyday I hope something will happen, worthy of relating to a reader. In any case, I'm confident there is enough here for someone to take a superior, which is to say, "critical" attitude towards and that's all that's needed, since any critical position generates another, more critical and so it goes, a linked chain of meaning.

for a reader. Hey, don't blame me, blame Knausgaard. I'm just a nobody. Are you a nobody too? [9]

Behind clouds, the moon changes her face.

25. Nov. 12   Another night, why am I alive and when will this end- the answer to that part, soon. It was Guy, who looked like nothing so much as the a*nimatronic* version of Gollum, peering under his steering wheel as he lead footed his big engined, boxy old Chrysler Cutlass (hand me down, natch, from dad) who said "this is one really weird planet" while I, in educated ignorance gassed on about how Kant's cant can't but Hegel's fables were able, the dialectic of progress when what I needed was ten inches of cold wakeup vegetable up my ass, the cucumber proviso, maybe that would have aroused me from the dream of reason. All that stuff, even the scholars, the guys who live their lives with it and keep it alive in books and articles and presentation at the conferences where they get laid if they are lucky, even they don't believe it, don't live their lives actually or cognitively by Kant and Hegel and Wittgenstein and Plato and all the time Guy was right, profound in fact because how many people can say it and really believe it – "the world is fucking weird" and don't think this is a case of talkers aren't doers – his rich reward ... op. cit.,"[51] I need some transforming drug but drugs are dumb

---

51   I may have implied that Guy was ugly; this is unfair. He was hideous, a by default humanoid form, a mass lumpously compounded of tumor and cat's hair ball with four tooth picks stuck in for limbs, a repellency so potent it was reverse charged, a making attractive to women (even infanticidel types like need not be named) who felt a duty, a biological imperative to bear whelp the creature into the warm fold of their humanity. He was also, in no particular order, a liar, a thief, a cheat, a baby-pated bully and a braggart and while I

– everybody knows that. I require some general specific, some all purpose tonic like that prescribed apparently so effectively by that one good Elizabethan doctor—Dr Foreman, what did he call his potion, Halek? Its various compoundings. hard boiled, poached, scrambled, coddled haleck...halek 69, halek Bendedick, halek surprise, over easy ... never enough halek halek haleck. All halek all the time.[52] [12]

First frost. No crickets sing.

26. Oct. 18 Drifting into a mistake here since I scorn that guy[53] that has issued the what 20 volumes (each 400 plus pages) chronicling his as yet on-going life, a self conscious exposition, a self-indulgent diary of daily

---

might rehearse a charity that conceives he might improve with age since he could worsen only by act of murder (which he often in my hearing wished on Israelis), I see no point in repressing a truth to dissimulate a virtue, to have you think better of me, his unluckily circumstantial friend. Take not my word for it; after a one year teaching gig at The Alabama School for the Arts, he received two reviews on the website GradeyourProf.com: "Nasty" and "A Real Sh*t", confirming condemnations that saddened me inexplicably. (For a full and fair adumbration of his better qualities, see my *A Book of Emblems,* available from Amazon and fine bookshops everywhere. All proceeds to animal welfare.) As they say in the Shakespshere "Give me my leave, for losers will have leave to ease their stomacks with their bitter tongues."

52 *Halek, hallek* or *haleck,* Forman's code word for sexual intercourse (usually with patients) in his medical casebooks. Among Forman's clients were Mrs Mountjoy (Shakespeare's landlady) and Emilia Bossana (1569-1645), the dark haired (half-Jewish), musical, witty, sexually active and moving in the right social circles woman whom A.L. Rowse has identified as Shakespeare's "Dark Lady", a piece of detection so apt that if it isn't true, it should be.

53 See Karl Ove Knausgaard, *My Struggle.* Great title for a political biography?

self conceit. Who cares? But yes, he was sick of the novel's conventions though I suspect could he have worked within them (he says he tried) he would not be so fatigued, in his case, artistic innovation, if you think his semi-fictionalized diary such, springing from artistic inability. Very common, I think. I thought of it all, including the comma splices, before he was born. What I'm looking for and want to make is the compelling text – like, as mentioned Va.Woolf's diary or Sam Pepys' or that tightly grasping biography, based on his sea log, of the mad, doomed yachtsman, Crowhurst. That moment when the reader says ah, this is neat, suddenly, against the grain of their expectation. [54] Or, at least a trail, a track of one person's divagatory thought. I must find my own path, which won't be, I vow to thee my denied and repudiated reader, a mere transcript of my thoughts. Granted, the interesting bits are made-up, okay as long as I'm honest about it and maybe I am. Actually, only the boring parts are invented, something I learned from Will James (not William), whose masterpiece, *Smoky the Cowhorse* is easily the imagined equal of his second cousin twice removed, Henry James' great novels, *The Golden Dove, Wings of the Ambassadors, What Maggie Knew, The Tragic News* and *Portrait of a Shady* which, I read compulsively from 1978-1980 in the New York edition.[55] Sic, or perhaps sick

---

54 The desired effect like finding a love letter in a book, or a diary under a floor tile, one of unpremeditated revelation, the delight of not minding one's business. Crowhurst (See *The Strange Last Voyage of Donald Crowhurst*) was a yachtsman in a transoceanic race who sailed in circles in one location thereby having to fabricate credible navigational positions in his log of his progress that were far more difficult than actual ones. He constructed an elaborate false identity that by virtue of investment was "true" while his true position was false, a metaphor of the voyage of human identify.

55 The issue is not whether this is funny (or not) or just the scabrous

monumentis. A lark if not a (w)rend. Time, I think, for sex.

---

manifestation of a facile and facetious self one-upmanship. Does it obtain art's defining grounding which is equivocation? In any case, the default virtues and vices are purely verbal, a texture not translated into screen play, film, or virtual reality. Not anything you can see; in other words, something you must think. And then, this just in, *a week before publication*. Back story: a friend had referred me to an agent in DC who, all but sight unseen, bought the rights to *Laminations* and my prior, *A Book of Emblems,* for $500, fine by me. She sold it to some guy in NYC for a modest markup ($650) and he to guys in London, "treatment consolidators", Goodwood Ltd. They buy rights to everything-anything, put brief plot summaries on their website, subscribers (writers) make a claim, get the whole text-manuscript, which they can develop and sell back to Goodwood (still holding all rights) and if Goodwood like it, they promote it – England is small, they know all the right people at the BBC, ITV, Channel Four, the independent producers and by god they sold the thing – transposed to Cambridge and brits, with stomach churning plot changes (the "me" figure, called "James", pursues "BF" and "Guy" in a car chase, they run a traffic light and are killed. James, who for decades is guilt ridden, composes a sad book of aphorisms that becomes a best seller. In the last scene, the film (now called combinatorially *The Book of Lamentations*) composed of ten eight minute episodes (each introduced by a voiced over aphorism), James, staring at a 1914 era service revolver, is clearly contemplating suicide but a cat jumps on the desk— the life force, get it? How do I know this? They had to phone and tell me. Some legal thing. So sure, they hope to get Ben Kingsley for old James, Ben Whishaw for the young one, Juliet Stephenson for older BF, Laura Frances Morgan as the younger, with Toby Jones as "Guy" doing his perfected Capote mannerisms, all under the directorial command of some superb smaller forces maestro like Dominic Cooke, Thea Sharrock or Bernie Montgomery. One of those films that debuts in Toronto and Tribeca, opens in Brit and east coast "art" venues and that maybe you hear about at a party in Hampstead, Georgetown or Cambridge (US) and you think you might see it and don't. The film people get paid, Goodwood and the producers make a little. I've my $500 and a "based on" line in the film credits you can't read and honestly, no complaints.

Once I stopped thinking about I mean wanting sex all the time (even right after sex) and when was that ... er, at fifty maybe, certainly not earlier, sex solicited in two modes, one in the morning, right after waking, a hard-on that would not be denied, a surging and irresistible current seeking a channel, blah-blah. Your normal maler, (see Norman Mailer). Or in mid-afternoon or very early in silk sheened evening, a gritty longing, sand in the machine, a rough running and shifting uneasiness, a dim lit Hades of the rasorial self, a hollow urgency that either set me out on long walks in any weather – and rain was best – or put my head under the pillow, words, phrases, locutions just floating up through the froth, the mode of poetry, when I did my best writing. Rereading (I had forgotten I had. No, slightly suspected.) Emma Tennant's *Burnt Diaries*, an account of her affair with Ted Hughes (tubes of squirted nutrition), fetching, candid, it is an honest account of her complicity, her self-seduction. (Let's credit that if only 10% his multitudinous lovers bothered to read even portions of his poetry, he achieved more readers than any other contemporary poet but no text will tell you that. Go Ted. To be fair, no one could land a poem about fish better than he). To her credit, in the case not in question, BF was not self seducing but the utter complete relentless and vastly inconsiderate if not cruel seducer. What a turn on, the phallic woman, the femme phatale. A jittery thoroughbred, beautiful lines, needs exercise, always in a lather, headstrong, not to be reasoned with. I call her now in a voice pitched to minor urgency, a nickering ..."BF, come!" And she comes (not, note, as a matter of obedience but of choice), always she comes. Conan, Conan the librarian. Conan say "This isn't drivel. It's journal. The drift is diff." If here and elsewhere you say I'm not being very nice, vindictive you opine, keep in mind I respect, admire, revere and totally endorse BF in her untrammeled personhood, a hawk never gloved but since, in the instance or instances, she treated me less than nicely, I return the favor and would better the instruction. I could forgive, condole, turn the cheek, meekly pitch my kicked pup tent in the moral high ground but to do so I must first needs surrender, take my medicine like a bad (in the taking, good) boy scout, furl my colour and show the callow flag and that I will never do. I'm no turn-the-cheek Dorothea Brook and never, in fact, was she.[56] (Then there is Shakespeare in his whining reed rather than strong stave mode, ever ulcerating over women and their fidelity, as "Master Brook" does in Merry Wives, and King Leontes in *The Winter's Tale,* Othello, or Hamlet, ever with his pole stuck in sexual mire if not the babbling brook, "county matters", recalling Rupert Brooke and his country house bedroom bingo, Peter Brook casting Louise Brooks as Lady ... (Enough brook jokes, we'll brook no more.) Yo, but one more surfaces ...

---

56 I am reminded of the beautiful poem by Stevie Smith: *"I always remember your beautiful flowers/And the beautiful kimono you wore/When you sat on the couch/With that tigerish crouch/And told me you loved me no more./What I cannot remember is how I felt when you were unkind/ All I know is, if you were unkind now I should not mind/Ah me, the power to feel exaggerated, angry and sad/The years have taken from me. Softly I go now, pad pad."* Conciliation and condemnation are both positions at rest; the mind that oscillates between them will be energized and enlightened, though ultimately thinking evens almost everything out into equal plausibility and valence: did the Civil War even happen? You hardly know or care, you didn't see it. According to the Chittamara or "Mind Only" school of Mayhayanist Buddhism

"There is a willow grows aslant brook ..." Oh, feel ya! Oh, tell, oh! If you want to read a nice book, try *Pilgrim at Tinker Creek* [17]

Not enough to wet the hooves of the dainty deer,
the mountain brook.
Must I brook your shallow love?

27. Nov. 6   I can easily anticipate my critics, if any bother: "conceited, self-centered narcissistic mean, facetious, embittered whining despite his claims of an enforced and encompassing compassion. Where are visions of beauty and gestures of nobility?" Fair enough but you have not considered my three hours a week at the animal shelter, cleaning out cat poop or my six hours of volunteer work at the library, back-ache making shelving or my half-day teaching Tibetan refugees English, and donation, when I was employed, of ten percent of my income to charities? Or the simple pleasure of being an irascible old man. Well, have you? Oh, you didn't know? So when, speaking of nobility, among real men and women, was ignorance ever an excuse for accusation? Now you know and can hopefully see that my complaints occur within a larger context, a life lived you know nothing about excepting what I tell you, okay? The dilemma, victims have no perspective on their victimhood, just is, as, until weightless in space, we have no angle on gravity and this not an effect, something subsequent, but integral, the injury itself. In that sense, it is "poetical" for no poet has any objective take on his own poetry; it just is, which is why there is so much bad poetry – poetry only the maker could love or pretend to in that public masturbation, the poetry reading.[57] And why all poetry grows out of injury, even if that injury is the beauty of the world. Take it (be hurt) or leave it (be stupid).

Been reading somebody's book about "Time", it hardly matters which, there are many good ones and it turns out, there are many schools of thoughts about time and you can spend a lot of time learning all about them and ultimately be none, the wiser about time, wasting time. Suffice to say, nobody really has any sense of time passing. What they have is present perceptions which they check against memories and *metaphorize* into "the stream of time."

No, it's not quite as bad as a fish's theories about water; we are smart but the ultimate reality of the thing escapes us, hence the various proposed explanations. On one account which is true in some universe, we die before we are born and our lives run backwards from our perspective, not from the spectators. So what is causation, is causation symmetrical? Moral implications of this: all those victims, millions of Jews and Slavs and Roma and queers collaborate to make Hitler a bad person. Which is about as perverse a perspective as I can image, excepting what actually happened. *New York Times* readers were polled, "If you could go back in time, would you kill infant Hitler?"(A version of the Dostoevsky question) and the results were even

---

57 Why, contrary to common belief, the poetry reading is inferior to a silent appreciation should be obvious; when a poet composes, he mentally "hears" each word in the fullest possible range of its tonal amplitude; when he vocally reads, he must choose and impoverishingly present only one of them.

thirds: one third can't say, one third would and one third would not. Now a few of the undecided third are perhaps being sophisticated. Killing Hitler may clear the ground for an even more victorious murderous race killer, a sorta Hitler-Stalin combo. But really, folks, basically you have to get over your everyday qualms, docile decency and suffocate goo-gooing baby Hitler. One shouldn't even think of allowing Hitler to live, he's gotta go, your moral nicety is an indulgence, and – these were New Yorkers! How many in middle America would let him live? I mean why rock the boat – we with our cars and houses and pools and sports and beer and whatever, it came out alright, alright? Eradicate Hitler and we might lose Elvis, heavy metal or Goggle.

Oh my god, scientists somewhere are saying alcohol is as bad for you as cigarettes, bad as hotdogs, worse maybe, more studies that would show it haven't been done, discouraged by big industry, governmental indifference. I have shortened my life. Granted, some drinkers and smokers are self consciously complicit in their injury, they know they will die and indeed must die, they need to move on, vacate the stage if the world is to change and need I say progress – and who, looking at history, can deny a gradual by no means consistent, hard won, hit or miss, progress in science and society? Want to live in Tudor times? You make what contribution you can. After age 60 you are giving less and needing more. Everyone knows they need to move on because if all those alive in 1880 aren't dead by 1980, we will never have well, the NFL and MRIs. We won't have room, mental or spatial. So yeah, a few drinks will harm you – and what harm is that?[58] People need to die. [36]

The light lessening, why does the spider sleep?

28. Dec. 8 I have always found it hard to get up, as long as almost I remember, back to age 12 (so presumptively, there was a time in childhood I don't remember when I did bound up, fascinating stuff), wanting to not to be conscious, to stay in bed, no energy and the weight of living pressing me down. These days I get up when BF does with the cat, a furry purry alarmed clock set at daylight savings time six. A bite to eat, some water, back to bed, BF and the cat go back to sleep, I watch the morning develop, counted the three of us in bed, our lifeboat floating on the sea of time, trees coming into shape, birds abouting, until the rosy colored morning clouds are bleached white by light and I get up the second real time, put the coffee on and by then, some light purposed breezelet has blown all mists away to open another bright day.

Very impressed with Ruskin's *Stones of Venice*. I get it, the workings of his psycho-complex like piston strokes, propelling him, his weird ur-Protestantism yet love of Catholic art and architecture, his respect for the working man but his skepticism of democracy, his quaint, untenable belief that faith determines politics vying with his real politic knowledge of men and events, his whole complex about women, a strange man who – as is frequent in such cases, to be forgiven –writes respiringly, expresses what amounts

---

58 Has anyone remarked on the perverse pride of we drinkers? "I am drunk, self- handicapped, and doing a great job of sitting on this stool, walking down the street or writing this novel."

to nothing, beautifully, a complex, fluid style that found its proper focus in Venice, as liquid Venice too conduced the style, his voice, quirky, opinionated but never vociferous. A few thoughts like this, then out, in fall and winter, to feed the squirrels who are expectant, twitchy tailed especially in this non mast year. [31]

Late summer, bees at the flowers' hearts, pollen drunk or dying.

29. Nov. 3   BF has possess me of, positioned me at the point of, impossible conundrum. On the one hand, I can't abide the place of her betrayal, I flee from it. On the other hand, it is the only place of authentic being – that it happened, that it was that way, my very specifically and exactly crafted downfall. I must affirm it, I cannot abide it. Likewise, it destroyed my simple sense of self, well-being and soundness; on the other hand, in breaking down the narrow frame, it opened up the world. What self went down? I was freed from my comfortable conceits and thrust out into a place not made for my self serving expectations, the real world where, feeling for the first time n*on-negotiable* pain, I could comprehend others', generating a true rather than contrived compassion.[59] Trade off. Pathei mathos, the tee-shirt. It gave me a theme, an argument when I was (and am) just strolling along, a happy well-adjusted chap whatever I may have otherwise implied

---

59   "The finest thing about betrayal is its ability to generate the intellectual motivation necessary to investigate the hidden side of others." – Alain de Button, *On Proust*. A curious observation, which read a second time acquires comedic possibilities.

in the interest of dramatic chiaroscuro.[60] Of course, she is sorry, so sorry. You have never seen a sorrier looking woeman on official contrition day, the moaning-morning of it, how comming in on all fours, she rises to her knees, clasps her hands and wails, forgive me, forgive me, her eyes glistening with tears, hair undone, distressed, rocking back and forth, barely dressed, just a carelessly buttoned white blouse that stops short above her long lovely legs. "I've been bad, bad, what CAN I do, forgive me, I'll do anything." We can see where this is heading. The usual compensations of the common melodrama. More than you want to know.[61] Exactly what you want to know and that the color of her frilly bedware, replaced annually from wear and tear, was/is bright bridal white. Sometimes I do see it, a vision of the entirety; in a model of static time ... all the slices of personal happenchance melded together, a dimension, the one "space" of consciousness where we have lived and loved. [27]

The most fulfilling thing, longing. The most capacious thing, this self, seeping through a hundred thousand flaws.

---

60 "The self expressed in writing is not the self that writes"- Proust. All of us possess depths that we attempt to activate by loves/hates, joys/griefs, commitments and betrayals, because without contents, the depths are voids.

61 The issue is older than sticks. Crowe Ransom to Robert Lowell (1927). "The family stuff is bad, like messages to yourself, with no public or literary interest. " I agree; the grotty grit of the private is not conformable to the forms of art and I am gratified that no incident of my private life has even once been subject to poemification. A journal – instinctual, uninhibited, dishabilimented, is another beast entirely, its exhaustive revelations as necessary and hearth warming as a bear's farts. [For "Crowe Ransom", read "Alan Tate" – ed.]

30. Nov 29   Saw *Spotlight* at the cinemaplex. Crisp script, good performances but low moral frisson, the good characters acting good in the interest of the good, the bad, badly in the interest of the bad. Great though, on the teamwork angle, how hard work and good hearts will get us there, a world of tolerance and adequate means for life for all along with cyber enhanced human capacity and yes, coming right up (wait for it) the genetic conquest of death. Worldwide, in historical terms, things are relatively good, never so many people so relatively well off. As *The Economist* reports, the last twenty years have seen fewer people killed in human violence that at any other time in history. So yeah, we might make it. But it all seems thin to me, a tissueated progress, a randomized good period; I don't think we will make it. Compare to *Wolf Hall*, the TV film – everybody flawed, More, Cromwell are a mix of self affirming good and evil. Yet think too, More and Cromwell at supper, they conceive of a world where doctors cure, you can fly from county to country, you can talk to your distant friends and relatives instantly, you can summon up a theatre, a globe like theatre of entertainment in your living room, wouldn't that seem just too fantastic to ever be real. Yet we did it. (And not just technical advance, better well-being makes better morality.) To smug cynics who doubt progress, I say, of course there is progress, at great cost and by no means straightforwardly. Nor is it fair to counter "Well, we haven't summed it all up yet." Well, it is never summed up, it is always a work in process. I should mention as an aside, the most exquisite thing about the *Wolf Hall* was the slow takes and long lingerings on everyday actions, writing on a piece of paper, a sip of wine, the touch of a hand, the doffing of a cap so that we see the pathos of every human action, all lost, even if recordable, down the funnel of time, each gesture gracious because instantly dissolving.

Weird, too realistic dream, I snapped and was expressing all the things I sometimes feel but never say (sic), that she was traitorous and trivial, that she has no real achievement in her life except successful betrayal of a friend that trusted her, that she has put me in the impossible position of necessarily, practically forgiving her while deep down her injury festers and said "I still see your beautiful poker face, lying."[62] She said "Oh and I bet you never knew that the night you dropped by suddenly and it was clear from my coat being on I'd been out I said I was looking at the blue moon and described it, "dragon clouds racing in the moonlight" when in fact I was just walking back, wet, from being with him. You never guessed." I shouted, "You think I want to inventory another lie?" And she said- you are right, it's over, I'm leaving- for both our sakes. At that I was stunned silent a while (fathomless dream time) and immediately felt devastated in the prospect of a life without her, no life. I begged her to reconsider – she was thinking about it and I woke up then to the cat pukeing. (No one knew the cat, innocent in its animality, was gravely ill.) Let it be recorded : we never quarrel or mention or muddy

---

[62] In a sense, one's deepest self is not implicated in this kind of suffered wrong, which signifies more than the obvious observation that "other people being jerks has nothing to do with me" and that complaints in such cases are always vulgar. Rather it has to do with our innate aptness for living, an imperturbable balance at the pivot of our being. That said, topical addresses on nobility always make my head spin. In the middle altitudes of life, it is better to grouse than to glide.

our daily happiness with stirrup from the old days. But something this once had welled up. [6]

"Yours faithfully" were his last words, addressing life like the close of a letter.

31. Dec.10 I should attempt it, *"The Bricks of Charlottesville."* From the low river plain, view to the west of blue grey hills that once were higher than Himalayas, through long generations of wind and rain, wearing down the rock that collected down slope, to become in time, sediments and soils, the retentions of silicate on this gradual geographic slope, deep clay loam, a red band compacted to depth that the settlers recognized, excavated and shaped, as they had at home, into units to be racked and kilned to form, even more than the abundant woods, the basic building material. Bricks, at first flatter, higher density slabs, later a lighter, more cubic and no less strong unit for what would be the most perfect (they say) ensemble of academic buildings in American, the long colonnades, an Enlightened frame centered on the green oblong of Jefferson's Lawn, sited on a broad slight rise that dropped, half-panoramically, to the misty south. Goes on for 100,000 words or bricks. Now anyone may "kick at life's pricks" but you'd be very wrong to scorn the bricks, blocks, honest clays, simple squares that tell an honest tale, an historic area, not quite ruined despite every well meaning effort of the last sixty years to make a vast Disneyish Jeffer-Palladisonian architectural theme park of brand name ("one hell**UVa** school") knockoff brick erections. [18]

32. Sept. 28 Near finished with Todd, liking Wollstonecraft much better. She needs, as she knows, occupation and hazardous engagement to prevent the pathetic-petulant implosion into ego, winging and holier than thouing. In Paris and Scandinavia, she is brave, energetic, a loving mother and overly besotted lover, painfully aware of the contradiction between her unrenounced feminist ideals and her all too human desires. Sad. The irony that her greatest cultural production is, arguably, her daughter, whose birth kills her thanks to the conscious indifference it not unconscious animosity (if Woman is the Other, woman giving birth is the ultimate Other) and brutally clumsy administrations of let us assume consciously well intended male doctors. The Elizabethan quack, Doctor Simon Foreman, let us note, was happily ineffectual with his horoscopes and herbs, doing if no good, no harm. Prone though, to inject his patients fem. An internist. A board certified gynecologist, inserting his diagnostic probe when patient positioned on a plank, on the ground, in a boat, against a wall. Which leads me, speaking of planks and surfaces … after I got a small, twelve tube oil paint set from an after Christmas catalogue sale, I have painted thirty-five 5 x 6-inch canvases. It has been an enlightening experience, informing (and informing on) my writing. While I strive for effects of complexity and multi-dimensionality, my work is visually flat and completely commonplace, a one dimensional composition of "added on" elements, addition not deepening. "Circumspice." My studio, a dusty, (graveyard of dry crickets) storage corner of the basement with dank spots and cold currents, portioned off with a partition of dark stained pine clapboard. In the sub light, it waved over me again, the old pain and I broke down and cried, 49 tears of 7 times salt before I pressed out one final drop and saved it in a tiny cosmetic bottle (belonging to BF), held to my cheek because such drops possess great alchemical potentiality.[63] Ju-Ju. Our games there, in the stale air, half light and confines, demanding artist and obliging model, randy-handy man, on-call rapist, no rescue. What fun. Darkness exerted into light. (Sick, you say? If it works sexually and is no crime? Get real.) Distill. [7]

"The most astonishing thing – to have lived these sixty years and often to have danced for joy."

33. Sept.14   Clearing to another too brilliant, too revelatory day. What are we, under this illumination? Reading Todd's superb biography of Wollstonecraft.[64] Love the name – one I'd commemoratively give a daughter "Eve Wollstonecraft Nelson", how's that for an adverse, incapacitating, doom-inducing moniker? But I have no daughters, none to become choleric rock musicians, nor at age 63 likely to have any despite my dad's siring a son at age 74, a working man was he who had not, it seems, wonked, enough. Late in the game, fourth and long, he went for the touchdown – and scored. Me, I aborted my girl-child.[65] I soul-sensed her, abort number one, my daughter; the second, a son sucked outta the womb, over the top boys

---

63   "As soon as you see the woman take a black colour, know for certain she has conceived and when the seed of the man embraces the seed of the woman, this is the first sign and the joy of this whole work of art. Therefore preserve a continuous heat and this blackness will appear and disappear through being consumed and as one worm eats another and goes on consuming until not one is left." – Paracelsus. Which is more or less what happened.

64   *Wollstonecraft, a revolutionary life,* by Janet Todd. 1995.

65   A Miranda shipwrecked in air, with no rights read.

and gals, never breathed but once the open air, killed in the sex wars ripped, RIP. Double minus. Poor little blighters, never had a chance. Wiper'd.[66] Defeated fetuses, died that we might live. Will her underdeveloped flotsam of a soul assail me in the latter time like a neglected kitten, a clinging, damaged demi-geist, mewing, "father, father"? I doubt it. Anyway, I've a fool-proof alibi: "Don't bother *me*.... "do it to "Julia", your mother, so called."[67] I've lost the thread here and my instinct – to follow the thread into the labyrinth, not out. (The Minotaur wasn't all bad, a bit of a bully, a rough neck, sure, but only doing his job.) Todd and I are congruent –Wollstonecraft is admirable – courageous, original and free-thinking, fighting against the odds, intelligent, compassionate, on the right side of history but also, a prig, a hard-ass moralist, an narcissistic egoist, a know it all, an intolerant bore ... all in all, an alley cat, scrappy and self-possessed, who god knows, after so brief a happiness, died horribly, doctors manhandling her soft insides. Washing hands wasn't best practice. I mean, women were dirty already, right? [Perfect thought for a downer day – thinking of all those women dying in agony and stink, from puerperal fever when, mostly, we're not talking big science here just a little lavation, women dying less when hands were washed, how all the big suites laughed at the guy (Sam Wise?) who put basins in the wards, typical man stuff "YOU don't tell ME what to do", it need never have been.][68] [11]

---

66 Likely pun on the name of the famous World War I battlefield, Ypres, pronounced by common British solders as "wipers."

67 The reference is to Orwell's *Nineteen Eighty-Four*.

68 Probably Ignaz Semmelweis (1818-1865).

Falling on the surface, raindrops disappear in a perfect circle even as the stream is flowing.[69]

34. Dec. 6 We took "the Hill Walk" today, which I am very fond of maybe because of its resemblance to the dry bald top hill in Tenn, with the broad views of the lush fingered valley and bottom lands, those hot summers of bee hum and banjo strum. All balderdash, where does it well up from, I was born and reared in a Norfolk Va. slum building, a two room "apartment" in an ca.1900 crumbling brick tenement that had a small pot bellied coal stove in the living room for heat. Today, speaking of welling up, I keep thinking of the sole nursery rime my mama taught me – and it wasn't one. After dad died, once a year, at Christmas she'd buy a bottle of sweet *Manischewitz* black berry wine (with, to this Christian child, the mysterious, attractive rabbi on the label) and drink it, a small glass a night between Christmas eve and New Year's. Some celebratory ritual on her part. Before she finished, she'd fall asleep with her evening newspaper (*The Ledger Star*, with its blue ink edge stripe for the latest-last edition) under the hot incandescent lamp, what she did most evenings anyway, her brain blanked out. But tanked up on her little glass (a small sized jam jar), she'd first recite her curious holiday rhyme "Once upon a time the goose drank wine, the monkey chewed tobacco and the horse went blind." I was fascinated by the mythic character of it, would recite again after she did, those bad, adult animals and

---

[69] In the notes to his translation (full bibliographic citation on p. 44), J. Hopkinds says in this, one of Rabbat's most famous ku, the raindrop symbolizes the person; the circle, individual consciousness, and the stream, existence/time.

the final suffering horse, the fine triptych of it, with the non-rhyming middle line. How I loved it, the high point of the holidays for a kid who had learned not to expect presents. Just about ten years ago, I looked it up online and learned, there are numerous variations but all have a middle line that rimes, most commonly "The monkey chewed tobacco on the street car line." Of course, my poor uneducated clueless mother got it wrong but I also think she got it asymmetrically right. Later, when I was older, I'd look on as she snored and wonder if she could be raped. Well, boys will be boys.

As to the Hill Walk, named for the university's Observatory Hill, the nearest high point for the 1890 era big refractor that still does the work of big astro thanks to the mile, half mile rough circumference of woods that surround it, no academic building or street lamplights to light blind the probing tube, and this our once a month destination from our house, the polite and prosperous academic neighborhoods, then though the ever more congested campus, a half hour to the hill's boundary, then a twenty minutes up slope the ten degree angle, twenty down the lengthened lessened incline and a half hour back home, call it an hour and forty-five minutes on a good day for three mile circuit which ain't bad given a figure I know, the mile in twenty minutes all day marching speed of Lee's army, young men in perfect pacing fitness, granted with thirty pounds of musket, ammunition short rations and water but factor in too our upslope; yes we have done and do well. None happier. [28]

It was disappointing, he said, to have crossed so many fields and never to have been struck by lighting.

35. Dec.13   Watched the Ian Holm *Lear*, a stylish high velocity version with exquisite (English) ensemble acting. Lots of lines cut in the American public television offering I was watching but maybe they were cut in the original London theatrical version in the interest of intensity and achieved, a fast, fluid presentation. Let me boast, I know Shakespeare as well as any professor and Lear leaves me unmoved, an eloquent tragic-existential vision that is unsuccessful as tragedy. A stubborn old tyrant, after various inhospitalities, dies, after a few belated hankerings for the welfare state; dies, still a stiff stick. Old Hickory. Various traitors are punished, so what? The Edgar-Edmund family drama sparks along but the entire thing lacks motion, the movement/development of characters (even if that motion is ever one of self- fulfilling destiny) A lot of uneasy antics. I recall Nichol, his assertion that Shakespeare knew the German word for empty, "Leer", and hence the Bard spins off with the repeated incipit word of "nothing", clearly balderdash yet this implication, mere chance association, becomes meaningful, a parody of verbal signification. And what does Llyr, the old Celtic word mean, anyway? Don't tell me – nothing? (Looked it up, means "the sea", the wasteful, the wanting.)

Learned this morning that my first boss in my first real job has died at age 92. By all accounts (including mine), a mild, pleasant, conversant man. Yet I had also witnessed the declining declensions of his smile that would end in a tight line of lips, jaw throb and a reptilian flush rising from the neck, how he would never change a decision having taken so long to arrive at one, a clinging stubbornness as if it was an inalienable monument of his otherwise not very evident virility; at this level, several rubs down, he was disagreeable. Devoid of friction, granted, a most pleasant gentleman, I can see myself, age 25, in the interview with him, on the edge of my chair, the weird monkey face-to-face of it, confident enough in my articulateness and utterly empty, without money, none other than student possessions (books, clothes), no definite prospects or ambitions or talents, the situation of the young generally whose indefatigable assets aren't vitality or mental flexibility but the necessity of youth. The fate of it sees one through.

Still in Venetian mode, reading a straight political history along with Ruskin's rhapsody, a sharp practiced, aggressive proud and avaricious state but aren't they all, Romans, Brits, Mongols, French, Russians, Americans, Chinese, the Venetians, possessed in their patrimony of only a few mud smacked islands and mosquito flats, more justified in their rapacity than most. Art excuses a great deal; true, they ransacked the terminally declining Byzantines but had the good taste to take the four horses, set them on the basilica's facadel platforms to haul St Mark's glittering chariot through all the tides of time. (Fine writing but since 1990 they've been stalled behind velvet ropes, spotlighted in the tourist thronged museum. Diminished to curios.) How much suffering was that worth? A lot, provided you aren't the one suffering. Read in the *NYT Book Review* an aphorism cited for its artistry, "A couple – a conspiracy looking for a crime." This is the kind I detest: plausible sounding, self–indulgent, self-satisfied, in its clever hermeneutic, with the allure of a stunt, a trick, not a truth, embodying one truth – the truth of the trick.[70] Slept quite badly last night and so fell into

---

70   Review in the *TLS* (no.5905) "With such frequent digressions, this author risks descending into self-indulgence." Okay, I get it. So

a nap, my deepest sleep in two years of living here. Yet I was a conscious of breathing, of being alive without a reference point of ego, without possessions or even the mental activity of a dream. Pure emptiness it seemed, what the Buddhists practice a lifetime to obtain.[71] Wonderful as recreation but isn't the joy of life the attainment not of "emptiness" (what a concept) but of fullness in all its manifold contradictions? [39]

The stream is crystal clear
that I must cross
clouding its waters,
to begin my journey.

I should have written this book inside out, a nonexistable volume to be sent to some small, independent (gov. grant dependent actually) press like Eve's Apple Press (Aurora, NY) whose printing run of 300 copies might have allowed me to unself-indulgently indulge maybe thirty readers. Nay, I'd rather stick my outrage to the screwing place and honestly rail. Question: Was Mahler, with all those zizzers, tooters, and six-foot bass hammers self-indulgent? Wasn't BF brighter, more beautiful, more duplicitous than Alma? Scherzo affectuoso.

71 Buddhists, their mediations, Christians, their prayers, Cabbalists, their exercises, all means to insight. My method, the historical mope. Every day the last eight months, I've gotten up each morning to contemplate Admiral Karel Doorman. He's stationed in the Dutch East Indies, far from his home in Holland where his wife and child live under Nazi occupation, he in operational (not ultimate) command of a little big composite fleet (scraps left over from the Dutch, British, and American fleets after the devastating Japanese assaults of Dec. 1941), a force too big to run or hide, too small to have any chance of defeating the main force of the Imperial Navy. Doorman gets up every morning, awaiting the order to attack, knowing he and most of his men will die, that every action he takes will be historically second guessed to confirm he is an incompetent loser. He doesn't want to rise but his whole life has been the acceptance of responsibility. Maybe today his chronic amebic dysentery will be milder so he can sit in the captain's chair.

36. Nov. 7   Watching *Grand Illusion* on the vintage movies show ... stop after an hour, the grand illusion being the premise that men were ever that humane, high minded, as if German guards, accurately mostly granddads, would be so consistently nice to Allied POWS with their own families starving from the British blockade. Bogus bonhomie. I recalled repeating my experience of 35 years ago when I tried to watch it with an almost identical fleecy host in front a faux fireplace pretending to be a home (which is where I am actually watching it and this sense of pointless repetition suddenly inspired a dire recognition that at age 63, I had arrived at my second childhood, oh I'm physically fine- note my obscenely geriatric sex (yes, as foresaid, more than you needed to know) but I was taking a long curve back to age ten, sex a strange new world ahead (now behind), me with no real interests in ideas or art or culture (waif of the white ghetto, what did I know?) a bit of a reader along uninformed lines, histories and sci-fi, totally clueless yet groping towards art, literature and music and now I'm back at ground zero from the roundabout route, knowing those things but I can't abide then, so that my entire life and those intense decades of intense, one might say desperate engagement with culture nothing but a divagation. I'm essentially back where I started (as is, alas, any nonexistent reader), without the tally-ho of sex, other male rivals and women a goal, I'm reverting back to my self-satisfied smug narcissus of a self. I haven't gotten anywhere, my project of improving self-transformation a delusion. Thinking this in bed that night, I felt more despair than at anytime since a friend's cat died. A pointless life, futile work and no children. One odd thing however, my dream that night, hard as they all are to relate, narrative being the air that makes them vanish at the contact but its very vividness preserved for a time its form allowing some kind of recordation; the object in my hands was an art exhibition catalog, the last item being a three quarters page color photo of a long Greek stele, with fours figures carved in that almost unbearable prefect Greek realism only the four figures, one seated were time and weather worn, rubbed down from their original relief and the figures in order were Karen my first wife, me next to her, next BF seated, and standing slightly off to her left Guy and it was Guy who had written a poem based on the image that ran a full facing page next to the illustrated one, words that from the first line (you can always gauge a poem from one line) depicted the timeless quality of the emotional situation he was in, verbally intense, complex but clarified like middle Auden, like Greek sculpture so that I was utterly impressed and moved and not envious because envy happens at lower levels, the middle altitude where everybody can fly – no this was very high, nothing personally to be jealous of because it could only be achieved by that person, the way you don't envy the horse head at the British Museum or the Art of Fugue, beyond personality and even in half- sleep, I realized this dream was giving the lie and the confirmation to my despair, confirmation that this was stuff I could no longer or ever obtain while aware too that this vision was generated by my brain – and that assigning it to Guy, was the best artistic gyre of allegory, the message: get up and get to work. Despair is often self-indulgence. Yet consciousness, like air in the tomb, eroded all the beautiful words, with only one phrase retained, like a shard, "one of the four, invisible…" suddenly he was visible and the four of us, were what, etched but eroding.

Nothing can convey it, only poetry, the irrecoverable poem itself of which a most imperfect copy, a bad quarto, would be this sketch drafted twenty years before ...

The House of Youth

Call it a drug den of hormones
where many came, stayed and went,
a place of young eyes and ears and hearts—
such hallucinogenically keen perceptions!
How to find one's individual way
down a corridor of turnings, strange pairings?
And then, only half learnt, our turn to leave.
That house cannot be revisited.
Torn down, that actual one, for a doctors' parking lot.
(Monument to unhealth and wealth.)
But I still can see its urgent rooms, furnishings,
not as from a place I've been
but to one I'm breathlessly heading.

Yes fine, but the narrative of despair was over-dramatized and the dream too long in the relating, this exercise in self-critique too imponing, a yesty collection of winnowed sentiments, in a word, waterflying. [37}

What bird is that, its wings beating? My heart, my heart.

37. Nov. 9   Leaf rakers come in two schools, those who rake along lines and those who make circles, long lines made by length long rakes along both sides of a line are, I think, most efficient but the humanly centered circles are more pleasing. For variety there is the rake waltz that makes an irregular heap. Looking up only about five percent of falling leaves have that beautiful slow gliding spiral falling. "Falling fall", a pretty phrase I was likely not the first to think of it. Nor of "Tao of Meow", a light, feline confunstion that would have earned me millions, blazoned on tee shirts, tote bags, coffee cups. Oh, today we took the cat to the vet for her annual check- up, the vet practicing a kind of genial formality, white coat and tie, is taking a genuine concern with cat health, has three cats of his own and not the society of dogs you'd expect. Dogs are better business. He strikes me as a ideal kind of guy, gentle but through with Storri, chatting to us (good bedside manner) the while. To devote your life to animal health and easing their pain strikes me as the highest kind of normal life – we aren't considering wacko noble self sacrifice here (Sidney Carton) and all the time I was also thinking of last night's murder – I've become a fan, "addicts" the network approvingly calls them, of crime TV, the two husband murderers, one strangled his wife with a barbell as she exercised, making it look like an accident, that it fell on her throat. Another, the man who slowly poisoned his loving partner too trusting to suspect him until he lost patience and when she was physically weakened from the low slow dosages, forcibly injecting her with a massive dose (antifreeze!) to quickly finish her off (her doctors had been for weeks, er, baffled) just to get her 200k life insurance award and they were regarded as "the perfect couple". Well, that's about the spectrum of male humanity (though women famously also poison). Looking at good Dr. Greg, intelligent, placidly (oh, by contrast, the demonic dark hair that ensnared me) blonde, clear eyed but clearly the trusting type, I wonder, is his wife faithful – has she done the natural thing – betrayed him?

A thing you learn; it's fidelity that's weird, exceptional. Cat checked out fine. (But this turned out a lie. Three months later she was back, to get a diagnosis of incurable cancer, with four months to live.) [25]

Rainy night, no thunder.
The thirsty earth is murmuring.

38. Sept.27   Consider a life, the conjunction of a certain spermatozoa and egg, being born in a culture, a language, in time, being in a certain place at a certain time when you might have turned the other way … people you meet and don't …given my own line of exhaustion and exasperation itself just a surface to my form of professed unbridled joy, I don't see what other verbal form I could have taken other than these episodic unstructured expressions, certainly not the manikins of fiction, other than the monolithic monologue…This silence, spoken of before going into, was I there already, I don't know, I knew it would come, I stay in it to speak of it, if I who speak, for how long I, not I could not say for what do I know of duration even as I speak of it, I say never and ever and never say never; I speak of the four seasons if they were four and the different parts of the day and night though, lacking sun, the night has few parts, parts you'd notice unless you were awake and maybe not then because whom has ever seen a midnight, words words words, the seasons must be, may be said to be similar, call it a fall a spring but we don't mean water, not exactly, it s appeal a matter of, really, a drift, the names they taught me. Columns of them, lists with images opposite, item picture of pig, sliced, equates hamlets, when in the end it's the silence, a few gargoyles in gloom. The ending end, the real void not the one I macerate up to the mouth, up to the eyes, that cover me but even the quiet falters, it goes on and on and on and doesn't. I have no explanation to offer nor to demand, one day, one night sometime in between maybe the comma will come where I'll drown for good, then the re-silence, the *Unnamable* ... the last cry "Will no one rid me of this troublesome piece?", kicking the bucket.[72] It goes on and on and on.

Lying in bed, waiting for the thunder – this too is karma.

39. Dec.14   Last night (various reasons to be explained) I was clawed back into personal darkness, human mental hell. So this morning, I had to take a make an overtly moral assertion: every new day is a space of possibility and enablement of our work; to be worthy of it is to see the pathos of beings in their living situation. The cultivation of compassion extended first to others but also, if we are to fully live, ourselves. And this not mere moral cheerleading from a simple Simon. Much have I wandered in darkness, fallen and raised myself up to fall again, always lower. What relieved and elevated me – sometimes a person, a project or a cause *undeterminable* which, for lack of any exact term, I would call grace. What I learned from Ruskin: that expansiveness of mind can encompass structure without construction. [40]

40. Dec.31   End of year. Spur of what – resigned exasperation, I sent out various batches of my poetry to twenty

---

[72] Very likely not the first conflation of Thomas Becket, saint ("Who will rid me of this troublesome priest?") and Samuelwise Barclay Beckett, author.

journals, a good round number for calculating the percentage of rejection. Will report.* Also, first book read into the new year, Bachelor on his version of "secular Buddhism". He spent over a decade in Tibetan monasteries, studying the high doctrines and then five more years in Korean Zen like practice and his conclusion : while the emphasis on compassion and mediation practices are valid, most of what he learned was esoteric, scholastic, ritualistic bunk, something I have long suspected. True of the kaballah also; it suddenly occurs to me –the Ein Soft's contraction of itself to allow finite existence is what we experience as space and time.

As to these entries generally, I found that the next day, while recalling the day's events in detail, I could not recall a single phrase of my description of them, they had no station in the nexus of meaning; in a sense this was both a strength and a weakness, words written on water. All the qualities of a late work, that lacking the vivacity and originality of beginning to middle period work yet radiating the cunning to be strange. You see this exquisitely realized in Beethoven's late quartets (which transcend their cunning) and the weird final plays of Shakespeare, *Pericles* being the perfect case if the Bard had done any more than offer a few lines to the true author, that brawler and baud

---

*(Out of 20 submissions, one acceptance from the only British publication, spoiling thereby the beauty of absolute rejection. As it is, I am The Five Percent Poet. There must be millions of us. It could be worse, could be 10%. However, it seems fair to give the last word to another such a figure, the Danish minor Rilke-clone, Laurids Brigge who writes in the preface to his second book of poems, *The Bridge* [1914], "To sit in the silent room of a modest house and gaze upon a warm strip of afternoon sun; to know a great deal about people of the past and to be a poet, oh, what a happy fate.")

master, Wilkins, as they stood drinks at *The Dark Lady* bar so let's settle for *Timon*, I mean *Cymbeline*. Which he didn't; late works and simply bad works can look much alike save for the silver trace of cunning. And while I claim the writing – an attempt to replicate the effects of history, its happenstances and inevitabilities, the grain of thought and action traced on the surface of time ("Enough fine writing." –ed.) I do not recognize the irascible old complainant with his facetiously moderated forthcomingness: I was never more than a man scratching, for that moment, the itch. To that extent, an innocent.[73]

And what was the purpose of the little pseudo haiku, *in italics*, at the end of each entry? I forgot to say. They are refutations.[74]

Perusing one's quarry, the tracks get fainter until they don't.

---

[73] And a lucky one. "What wouldn't we have given for a life of ordinary misfortunes and heartbreaks!" — Mrs. Mandelstam, *Hope Against Hope*, p. 19.

[74] All the zen-like items were selected and adapted by the author from *A Bowel Full of Emptiness, the ten thousand tails of Roshi Rabbat,* compiled by His Eminence Kelso Mungo PharLap, translated by Jedediah Hopkinds, Triple Crown Press (an imprint of Snow Lion Publications, Ithaca, New York, 2014.)

Selected Poetry

Fates of Exchange

The soldiers, shifting in ranks to see the gifts,
grinned but Cortez, ever courteous and grave,
bowed low in acceptance, noting how easily
the Indians wore gold – necklaces, arm bands, lip plugs
that would buy estates in Spain, stables of stallions,
a pale Infanta's bridal hand.

The envoys, Montezuma's noble kinsmen,
were proud, seeing in what was laid down not submission
but proof of power, their city bestowing such rarities,
"shadows of the gods" they called them, capes and cloaks
made from "life-green, most green, what turns in the wind
turquoise, emerald", feathers of the forest dweller,
    the shy quetzal.

25 Vendémiaire, An II

Hoarse from question and denunciation,
the Tribunalists quietly flourished their verdict,
sent the woman, bereft of husband, children
and all Versailles's pretty things, back to her bed of
   biting straw
where in half-sleep's delirium it seemed a brocaded servant
stepped down a mirrored hall so that she must set her
   Age of Reason smile,
take from his white fingered hand (light split by the
   barred window)
the beribboned proclamation of the day – execution at
   noon.
This she foresees almost contentedly, as if a last levée
but the lurching ride in the uncovered cart,
the streets coiled into one vast animal,
its multitude of mouths opening with a roar.

Framed

I remember the grief, a period thing,
coeval with certain hats, hemlines, headlines,
cars with fins.
Now we know, pro and anti Castro Cubans,
Texas oilmen, reptilian Mafiosos,
the CIA, the KKK, cold-cocked husbands,
all were gunning for him that day
and have told us why, with what good reasons.
So many shots, so many Mannlicher-Carcanos …
bathetic as a ballad, Kennedy's head explodes,
at the center of every plot, Zapruder's rose.
All dated, all fades.
What stays fresh and strange
is the ever spooling reel of doubt,
a pale man between heavy deputies;
a reporter pushes his question, a microphone's barrel –
"Did you shoot the President?" Oswald's words rerun
"I'm the patsy, I'm the patsy."

Celebrate V-E Day with Ike's Colleen Driver

After the Germans signed,
our Allied stars slapped backs
and shedding with every camera's flash
the worry that made them thin, you could tell
how they'll age in the easy occupations their nerves
have yearned for, the soft campaigns.
Tonight, reveling in our chateau's moonlit,
jazz amazed gardens, they'll aim only champagne,
command just squads of waiters, grope along the garter
   line.
Here surrender holds.
But in the black forest a sniper, some Nietzsche reader,
thumbs his Mauser's bolt and waits. A farm boy
clumsy in his boots from years of bare feet trips
a mine – its malice goes deep, it happens far away
while defeat is always what's nearby that can't be helped;
for me – the general who sleeps in my V and returns
a hero to his quiet stateside wife.

The Peace

Was it like this –
the concuss of the last aimed gun diminishing,
crowds surging in famous streets,
cities loud with light and victorious couplings
late the next day awakening
to find their uniforms thrown off, estranged,
the grip of orders slipped and so they rested,
entirely at ease but for their straining to find
a familiar threat in the morning's hollow.
Was it like that –
our history of inflicted defeats
ending in this miracle where we both have won
and smile like statesmen at the treaties?
Days pass in a secure peace, for instance now
as we chat, cool atop the sheets, such friends
everything can be asked, be answered
except this – Do you miss the hard times?
their fact and metaphor the minutes just before
when I sized you up, we grappled
and were merciless in our movements,
making not love but war.

Feldgrau

In the twilights of his mind
he never left the trenches.
But professionally, he moved on,
there was much to learn –
mechanized, combined operations.
He married the Graf's youngest daughter
and soon came little Erica and Hans,
a succession of grey garrison towns,
field manuals composed, mastered.
In time, transfer to Berlin and promotion to staff.
a relief not to be a line officer –
having to police the streets,
breaking heads of Reds and strikers.
The country needed a strong leader,
a Hindenburg, a Hitler.
In middle age – a champagne gush of victories;
The Ruhr, Austria, Poland, France.
Sitting in the café, he watched the Parisians,
felt a satisfaction that was deeper
than a job well done, than his new uniform
(no longer Colonel but Herr General),
as if after shouting, he had at last been understood,
as if a difficult woman had finally come.
The sun warmed his wine. Light winked in a vase.
How good to be alive in the spring of 1941.

On Reading Manstein's "Lost Victories"

Above the glittering debris fields, the Benz Star rising,
bands back in the beer halls, stocked shops;
from retirement's bungalows,
the field marshals are again maneuvering.
"Dear Colonel-General,
thank you for your letter
describing the retreat of Army Group B.
If you are ever in Kassel ...
my account will appear in England
with an introduction by Hart,
their Panzer man."
The book I hold in hand, delightful
with detail and bluff, soldierly deceptions –
"Behind the in-leaf saplings of the state collective farm,
our Jaeger groups lay in wait."
"I knew of no crimes behind our lines,
my oath to Hitler I could not break."
A good dinner rumbles in my gut –
new reinforcements but I nod off
under the reading light's heavy siege.
Words fall out into letters,
long black ranks on life's white page,
like soldiers, like graves.

Singapore, 1940

In the two seasons of humid air – monsoon and high summer,
it hardly seems wise to worry. Newsreels glower "war clouds gather"
but end with an anthem and "Britain stands committed."
Reinforcements have been dispatched: Arthur Ernest Percival,
the new General Officer Commanding, was tops at Tactics School.
Admittedly, in tropic duty uniform (shorts and over the calf socks),
his is a stature more scout masterly than Field Marshalsome
which may – like the vast naval base empty of capital ships –
convey a kind of confidence and give potential enemies pause.
It may, but readiness assessments are undertaken anyway.
As opinion divides over the aeronautical ability of the oriental eye,
its handicaps of shape and shade, the verandas at Raffles Hotel
open onto the same fine views – Albert Square, the opalesque bay.
Around the round tables, beneath the paper lanterns, it's the usual chat –
money, politics and that most local of governances, who sleeps with whom.
Lights burn late too at Fort Canning. After a rigorous day of war games,

officers stand down, their underarms stained. Today,
India Brigade fell back.

Tomorrow, it regroups, counterattacks alone a line –
Percival moves a marker,

fingers a map – that runs through a rubber plantation.
Like the one

he toured when he first took command. Thousands of
trees planted in ranks.

The light was grey beneath their thick canopy. Anglo-
Dutch Michelin

arranged a demonstration. Squads of brown men,
machete-armed, fanned out.

In minutes not a figure seen; only trees slashed, bleeding.

Afterwards

The next day, they took the woman to the place of bitterest fighting,
to the bodies scattered like outbreaks of rock, clumped like storm slashed timber.
It was hours before she found it, the scar blazing the twisted, hacked at leg.
So they hefted him for burial, Harold, her bedmate and king, his face pulped in.

The common Saxons stayed, grey or white in the cloud broken light.
Ravens pecked at eyes and mouths, weapons were gathered.
A few prisoners, roped and shivering, were led down the beaten slope,
through the changing groves where leaves, bright blades,
rasped and glinted, voiced the wind, strange tongues fluttering.

Pacific Bathic

A reconnaissance team, we were landed to watch the straits.
No relief came. On the airwaves, tiny words, English,
 Japanese interweaved.
Dial lights dimmed. After many bright days, rain.

Iwo died from fever. Saito complained of cramps.
He set out for the mainland on a driftwood plank.

Weeks, months, the knot slipped down the calendar stick.
Each year, I place a stone upon the silent shine, the radio.
Days, I check the fish lines, levels in the water barrels.
The surf beats. Nights I try to sleep.

Today, a tower breaks the misty band of sea and sky.
A merchant ship beyond the reef.
Plainly painted on its prow, our flag's red and white.

The war had gone far from here.
It stayed in my dreams, mixed with women and a
 newsreel I'd seen.
The Emperor riding a stallion became the sun rising
 over sacred Nippon.
Black rays reached across the ocean, our Co-Prosperity
 Zone!
All morning I have watched the sailors scamble like
 crabs, like lice.
Now the launched boat nears. Sweeping the radio top clear,
my hands three times rise "Banzai, Banzai, Banzai!"
Years are islands, stones sparkle in the sand.

Bletchley Park

Cloud shuttered light and slaps of wind,
the rippled pond and one cold swan,
these we accept, nature's clear text
even as we interrogate the rain-pooled drive
that once was thronged with olive-drab official cars;
the vacant mansion echoing in our footfalls
its memories of generals and boffins,
the huts that were upstart, pungent with pitch,
dilapidated now into a barrow-like belonging,
where in a brightness intensified,
behind blackout curtains, a man, a woman
stare at randomized letters
looking for a way in, an intuition,
as if playing chess against a grand master
whose game has this weakness –
faced with one improbably correct attack,
his defense becomes predicable, this, then that,
a position cracked as decryption machines clatter
and dawn leaks in, the day watch entering.
Now, a half century later, what remains
is what can be read in any history –
"the best minds enjoyed recreational maths,
chess, puzzles, amateur theatricals"
or learned from the badged, bereted guides
though today their words are wind-blown,
scattered, as magpies, sheltered under the eaves,
chatter in old, unbroken code.

Meditation

It's numbing
thumbing through *Der Spiegel*
for choice pics of atrocity;
even if these hieroglyphs of death-debris
grime the pages' glosses,
even if my eyes are sharp as stick-pins,
it still may take hours to find
enough cut-rate tortures and basement hits
to stack my skewered brain
and make the Breugel ghetto where
decorated rapists (needles through their skins)
can pin women down in historical settings
Berlin, the Belgian Congo;
this is just the recreational aspect
when, really to see we're raw material for disaster
is a meditation on mercy that makes me
the kind of man I am – any panhandler's reliable dope,
an addict of self-sacrifice
who writes the UN asking them to stop atrocities
sending him deeper and deeper in.

Stern Ornament

The carvéd figures turn to us,
twisted in wooden whorls of pain;
mouths agape, their cries have rushed out
leaving this vacuum, this quiet.
Note the lion's underside, he's been "cropped"
and the unicorn, mere horse now, brutally dehorned.
Still, dutifully around the circular motto
"Honi Soit Qui Mal y Pense" they stand,
their story on the gallery's laminated label
briefly told: 1667, DeRuyter's raid
upon the Chatham docks, the English flagship
(Royall Charles) unmanned, surprised,
its long becalmed haul to Holland.
There the laying on of hands,
the breaking off of the enemy's emblem,
its four centuries of slow captivity,
since 1900 hung high like an altar piece
in this still cell of the Rijksmuseum,
even a bench provided for contemplation
of the force that lies behind all we do –
that frame it as we will, as karma or the chromosome
moves and moves on like a age of sail,
leaving in its roiling wake, moods, memories,
a flotsam track of artifacts, for example –
this stern and gelded ornament, suspended as monument
yet transmitting across history's dead seas
pride, determination, the grief of action
as we sit and shift, shallow draft vessels that have caught
   a trace of wind
and pull against our chains.

Fort Warren State Park

Where was meaning on the fortified island?
Was it on the parade ground, a bright vacancy
that strained to hear above the seas's drum
the last, the next barked command?
Or in the facts of history, here generals
of the late confederacy were imprisoned.
Was it in the layering, the salt marshes
surveyed and drained, the granite tones
stacked behind wind strummed mason lines,
the days defended by these cliffs and canyons?
Or was it in our trying to comprehend the bored,
ordered lives of the garrison or looking at our own,
late afternoon tourists fanned out from the crowded
    ferry,
in our seeing how in each case studied
something was missing and our thinking that this,
added to what we did see, must be the meaning.

Aphorismen

Aphorisms

"The aphorism, something I meant – once." Don Patterson

What's discreditable about every religion is that on the fundamental issues they have stopped asking questions and are confidently providing answers.

To have no interest in pleasing anyone is evidence of uniqueness of vision. Catering to even one appreciator demonstrates a sad decline in originality.

To insure urban and personal renewal, it is best to build on unreliable foundations.

Your friends won't tell you the truths that hurt and your enemies won't tell you those that help. They are the same truths, the ones you must need to know.

There's magic in the alchemy of converting pain to art even if the resulting object isn't gold but a lump of sluggish lead.

The two horses harnessed to the chariot of achievement are "Ambition" and "Disappointment". They hardly ever pull together but one will generally follow the other.

Buddhist lamas are justly revered as masters of high esoterica, experts in extreme mental development. Nothing indicates they are especially good at the hard thing: managing the desires and careful responsibilities of the ordinary person.

Forgiveness, he knew, was something you do for yourself. So, altruistically, he proceeded to revenge.

If we could escape death by eschewing sex, all of us would sign on. And nearly all of us would violate the contract even at the penalty of death.

Sexuality is the dream of life. Sometimes we listen to children and the old because they are awake in ways the prime time adults never are.

The false lover endows you with the knowledge you do not want. This is the only real kind; everything else is mere information.

The platitudinous statement "art must give pleasure" is non-controversial provided it is conceded the pleasure doesn't have to be pleasurable. Art is like sex; the point isn't pleasure but gratification.

Having critically appreciated the work of my teachers, I am ahead of them. Except that, allied with time, they must already be beyond their last work (where I am). Unless they aren't, having already fallen from their never secured crest to leave me in possession of a slope where to advance is to go downhill.

Few things are easier than talking nonsense about art and numerous careers have been based on nothing else.

Keats – "Poetry should come as naturally as leaves on trees." *Naturally* does not mean *easily*. In spring, trees ache with the labor of their forthcoming green.

A certain type of victim takes this solace: "Getting involved with an adulterer, an embezzler, a liar, what was I asking for but betrayal, fraud and lies?"

Nothing better indicates our abysmal ignorance than when, after the severest personal violation, we ask "how could you do this to me?" as if we were worthy citizens of a just universe.

Camus says "Doubts are the most intimate things about us." This is humane. I say pride is the most intimate thing about us. There's always the weak point where our bright armor links up with ego and that is where the dagger strikes. Nothing is more intimate than a wound. Which becomes a new kind of armor; one is impervious to all shorter stabs.

We could live a million years and the most fundamental question would still be what to do with our lives. Death is life-enhancing by encouraging us to solve the problem within an experimentally realistic time span. Perspective generated by the vanishing point.

After witnessing two or three deaths, one is capable of anything. Which is why, having packed off dying to hospitals and hospices, removed it from the streets and marketplaces, people are milder, less inclined to incandescent acts of cruelty and compassion. For society, this is a good deal since death is more likely to incite Borgias than inspire Buddhas.

Much of what we consider "intelligence" is rapid mental energy, setting the speed of our definitional lariat. High intellect that is sluggish escapes it entirely.

When is it right to take a knife to a gun fight? Writers are of two types: those that write for everyone and those that that write for no one. The former have a 99.9% rate of failure (even such vastly popular authors for the adolescent mind as Tolkien and Rowling reach only about 10% of available readers), the latter a 99.9% success rate. The situation is very roughly analogous to an anomaly in dueling: the man who selects his pistol in a firearm duel demonstrates his endorsement of the process; the man who asks for a sword, his critique.

If forceful enough, criticism has the effect of hammering one into a compressed position perfect for springing the next advance.

Tip for writers. It was only after I took up painting that I understood the superficialities of my expositions. I could *see* them.

Too long for an epitaph … "to be twenty and a poet is to be twenty; to be forty and a poet is to be a poet; to be sixty is to dream of being twenty and a poet" … *too short for an obituary.*

Lexical Rights Advisory. Readers aggrieved by consumption of previously appearing propositions may have right of compensatory recourse under the following terms and conditions. Complaint parties should specify prior encountered statements by page and placement in the author's earlier published books, Compensation will be awarded at the rate of one cent (U.S.) per repeated aphorismic unit on a onetime, one redemption basis, subject to a fifty cent (U.S.) deduction for processing and handling. While made "in good faith", the above tender does not constitute a contract, guarantee, redemption or promise to pay in the legal sense and establishes no obligation, moral or fiduciary, on the author who is the sole arbiter of all claims and of any dispute arising therefore with all normal and customary rights of non-compliance. This offer, herein known as "the offer", as and if iterated, replicated or reproduced is not itself a referent object under terms of "the offer." Claims may be made, via email, including notarized electronic signature and federal tax filing number to: Egent4@hotmail.com. Or sent in writing to 1641 Rugby Ave., Charlottesville, Va 22903, USA, Expires 9/1/2017.

The pace of technological change is so swift and the pace of writing so slow, all "creative writing" is now historical fiction.

Irremediable from the past, injury and defeat; yet I live. Inevitable in the future, death; yet I live. What is this present "I" – a thing pulverized, pluralized, hard to kill.

It is not so much Nietzsche's "what doesn't break us, makes us" as what impedes, speeds us.

Drive a stake into the heartwood and the bole may mend around the injury, meld about the rod so that even if by metallic conduction the tree is seared by heat and haunted by cold, it would not change being the hard-hybrid it has become. This is a parable.

It is good to meditate at night, just before sleep, on the prospect of one's dying in the next twenty-four hours.* One has, perhaps, only a few hours left to express one's best virtues, discard encumbrances (bitterness, regrets) and do good work in the world. The lived day, unfolding, seems like the purest grace.

You know there is reason for hope when the old king, having leered into the abyss, looks up to say "Let copulation thrive, I need more soldiers."

The "change" in a man: when what was the little dictator of his body just lolls around, a private waiting for orders.

Corrida. In the ring, the bull receives an excellent education. Pity he's killed by degrees and can't use it.

Because some say there are gods, angels, platonic forms and others say there are no gods, angels and platonic forms, our best philosophy is an open grasp of contradiction as when in dreams we are both here and there, speak to one person who is two, see a small, inquiring animal that is absolute cat and definitive dog

---

*[Some day, this will turn out to have been a 100% probability.]

I only credit an afterlife as an impossible subversion of tenses, as the place where we prayed, successfully, that we might be born.

Our intuition of an afterlife is like our talking to dead friends in dreams; we sense something isn't right but find it compelling because of, not in spite of, its implausibility.

As regards love, marriage, parenting, indeed life generally, what's important are the simple things – simple things that are often difficult.

As a writer, he was seriously disabled by sincerity.

Sometime around the year 2000, writing a book became like hand casting a horseshoe, a practice of value in certain niche vocations (dressage or academia), but in terms of society at large, something relegated to a fundamentally antiquarian or hobby activity.

The most discouraging thing after a hard night is hearing the birds singing their paeans to the inevitable day. The most encouraging thing after a hard night is hearing the birds singing their paeans to the renewing day.

Death is a mystery we cannot understand; a greater one is the expiration of love. The person you would have given your life for is now one you don't even bother to cross the street to avoid. What chemistry makes these hard hearts?

The Perfect Hurt. The damage must be real enough to deform the natural egotistical conceits ("I am worthy, lucky, winning, attractive, right") but not so destructive, as is often the case, to annihilate identity. Tending the injury, one acquires depth and maturity that is the basis of real (rather than facile) understanding and sympathy. While one should resist viewing this process too self-congratulatorially – "*Now,* I am wise, compassionate, etc.", don't worry; life always has a way of ballasting such resilient buoyancy.

Ah, Shucks. The perfect book for me is not a beautiful verbal animal (Rilke's private unicorn or indeed his entire lovely corpus) but a hard, almost disagreeable excrescence one cuts thorough in increasingly desperate (and diminishing) expectation of the glistening pearl.

Overheard at a Hampstead party. " The minute he died, his poetry seemed better to me; it had lost its superior tone, it was more like words chalked on stone.

You know you are dealing with an interesting thinkers when you eagerly anticipate their responses to persons and concepts they can't have made because they died too soon;

Schlegel on Schumann, Wilde on Relativity. Suddenly the responsibility is yours — to bridge the gap.

Macbeth, appraising the hags' prophecies, concludes they "cannot be ill, cannot be good." In regard to the supernatural soliciting of art, Macbeth the critic would have said "cannot be false, cannot be true". Art is the great equivocation; the witches Shakespeare's closest conjuration of artists.

People are petty in the sense they are not intellectually up to the problems of existence. As all artists are persons, we should not be surprised that most art is trivial.

We are mistaken to say our lives are too short (unless from accident or disease, they are). Short compared to what, a rat, a cat, a horse? What is short is the scope of our lives. We sense vast time before and after, conceive of millions of unfathomable fates. Our personal expanse is small. In that space, we curate the present and the past. What experience could possibly qualify us for such a task? For that, our lives *are* too short.

Most people just want to be happy. A few want to be hurt and won't be contented until they are. Happily, the world is so constituted they are certain of being gratified.

It must be a common fate, death drives you to distraction and those distractions are the death of you.

I wasn't disconsolated by my rival receiving deserved praise from real persons when all my commendation was from persons I'd imagined because my fictional admirers were more beautiful and insightful than his real ones could ever be.

Certain events so determine a life they must constantly be revisited if one is to live authentically. Yet the range at which they illuminate is also where they incinerate. One is in constant oscillation between safety and identity. Persons in this situation will be least at ease with the fixed positions of conventionally and are, to that extent, artists.

We gather our life's gems and dark pearls. They are non-temporal, solid conceptual objects. If we string them together in narrative to make a kind of necklace, meaningful as any made thing, Claude Simon and other experimental writers are right too to loop the strand back and rearrange the facets of event since, in no particular order, we finger them daily for the intensity of the touch.

I am often tempted to say to my Buddhist friends "The West also has a complex system of mediation. It's called literature."

Authenticity of the death certificate – the one document you will never have to prove you've earned.

At the reading, the poet articulates each word he has written with a reverence and self-adornation that makes one's teeth ache. Words deserve our respect but spoken in our mouths, they gravitate to common use, asking for nothing more than honest, unaffected utterance.

A formula for history. It feels good to be good but it feels better to be victorious.

True enough in that old adage type of way, "it rains on the both the just and unjust" has the wrong moral emphasis. The real injustice is the sun shining on the just and unjust equitably.

We are fretted instruments, designed to be sounded to our depths.

The genuine gentleman regrets being unable to challenge himself to a duel.

He had the look of one who had been slapped awake and couldn't forget it.

That our sense of self is so self-evidentially an illusion is yet the greatest indication of its meaningfulness and validity.

That language, removed from its usual syntactical situation, could emit special meanings ... I sensed a resonance in words that, relieved of their usual grounding, might flourish in lower gravity, as satellites in space unfold into life. There was a million to one chance it was so but in that other place, there might be a millions of chances, one for each word. The most "poetical" thought I ever had, I was determined to test its strange physics even in a laboratory as modest as a verbal kitchen because cooks, too, are physicists.

That the glib critic can plausibly assert that poetry is less significant than almost anything, including spectator sports, indicates the question embodies a category mistake, as if Bronze Age tribes were asked to choose between an ingot of metal and the Theory of Relativity. They would have to be an entirely different kind of people to choose the latter. In a sense this is what poets are saying – we would have to be an entirely different kind of people to choose poems over bonds, only we are already if only we knew (and only poetry can instruct us in this self-knowledge.)

At current rates of progress, we are no more than fifty years away from techniques of total genetic repair and the conquest of death. Then begins the Wars of the Doses because the poor will endure anything except a world where the rich never die and the rich tolerate anything except a world crowded with the immortal poor. (For those that fall short of the fifty years, there is the consolation that a world without death is more likely to be hell than heaven.)

Much less than the scope of my living mind, what will survive of me is this abstract of words, a conundrum we artists are always resolving to solve.

Being rather slow on the uptake, I took a while to recognize that the best part of most books is the epigram introducing a chapter.

Turn of the last century (2000/2001) architecture: beautiful prisons, penitential museums, the aesthetic stage of storage.

City: a moral theatre where the script, Art, is written after the fact, a civitas of sound and fury signifying something. Only culture distinguishes "urbs" from hive, being from bee.

Brutalistic buildings are "classics" because like the bunkers, flak towers, and submarine pens that inspired them, they have the power of aesthetic endurance, never looking any worse.

The perfect inoculation. In love, those that betray you confer great gifts in the act, the chiefist that they can never again *exactly* betray you. Such inadvertent generosity should never be despised.

Rationing. On a good day, I may have one entertaining thought. I've known people who have ten an hour; at that rate they seem like nothing worth recording and so slower wits have a kind of "handicapped" advantage.

Every poem is guilty of the gravest crime – existence, its only possible expiation being the full confession and transcript of transgression, the poem itself.

Hamlet, princing around Wittenberg, is the kind of sport who would kick a puppy out of his way and make a pun on "heeling" to the delight of his hanger on, hang-dog pals, Rosencrantz and Guilderstern.

To say heaven is communal and hell is personal is to describe the heavenly and hellish aspects of both locations.

Twelfth Night. Count Orsino's desire for Olivia is faux but he is aware his life is easy and superficial; there is nobility in his contriving a passion to acquire gravity and grief.

Pornography always has a tired, "been there" if not exactly "done that" aspect that is its most addictive satisfaction.

Geriatric sex: children playing dirty again.

Since most people are uncomfortable with untruth, we suppose we can detect lies by strain in the voice, too many blinks, a looking away. But some people are at home in falsehood and these, the great liars, are only betrayed by naturalness and ease, the signs among the multitude of truth.

Conjoined with our animal egotism ("I want, I say, I am") is the almost correctional thought "I am not worthy of the beauty of the world."

The worst thing that can be said of a work of art isn't that it's bad but that it is banal, keeping in mind there is nothing to prevent the future from finding it "typical" and revelatory.

Short essay on boredom. Some authors are born boring (Broch, George Moore), others achieve boring (Joyce in *Finnegan*) and some, over-promoted to an exposure their minor talent cannot possibly satisfy (Elizabeth Bishop, Geoffrey Hill), have "boring" thrust upon them. But "boring" is not a monolithically negative thing. Beckett's "borings" are sad-amusing, Tolstoy's tiresome anti-great man tirades ("*boring*", in *W&P*) are provocative-annoying; Proust's circumstantial obsessions function, almost in spite of themselves, as chiaroscuro and engagement. We have not yet sounded in their depths or varieties, the bottom of literary boredom. A book, itself embodying the strange physics of tedium, is surely forthcoming.

"Made in China" is the most common phrase printed in (post-Hastings) English. Not one person in the cultivated courts of China and India even hears of the obscure skirmish, a few thousand barbarians knocking their brains out on the lea shore of an insignificant Northern island.

Because humans are complicit in their own misery, animal suffering is the greatest argument against a loving god. It's not enough that there be a canine heaven where the dog doesn't recall his pain. The animal you see whimpering must never have suffered. Which is impossible except for Him for whom all things are possible, including the impossible subversion of time. Despite sounding like a routine sermon line, the idea is high, attractive and one understands as if standing on the edge of a cliff why so many have gone over the edge.

Unless we posit a paradise for cows, pigs and chickens, this world is a terrible place where the only thing that matters is who eats and who is eaten.

Shylock would not have traded the ring given to him by his deceased wife (and stolen by his daughter to purchase a trained ape at a party) for a "wilderness of monkeys". What is that wilderness? A vast natural order, a biosphere of thousands of acres where branches thrash and monkeys howl. It is also the alienable parlour of Venice, any society loud with jabbering simians. The wilderness of monkeys is the world.

The best way to disconsolate your enemy is to smile in their presence. This explains why every workplace has a cadre of hardcore grinners.

Roses have thorns, cats have claws. At the highest level, self-defense is integral to beauty; the lover who with a word or glance can inflict a wound.

After two thousand years of Christian instruction, it's not that hard to forgive those who trespass against us. We are not yet ready for a more intensive humility: asking the trespassers to forgive us.

One of those appointments that can't be refused though one had hoped and, perhaps, deserved better. There's little gain and no glory to be gotten out of Judea but new Procurator Pontius Pilatus is conscientiously determined to make the best of it.

Despite his chronically low grade dyspepsia, Edgar Lee Masters is justly prized for some of his Spoon River transcripts, as when he records Jonathon Somer's debate club challenge to Mr Tutt : "Before you reform the world, please answer the question of Pilate, what is Truth?" (Masters might have added, "And trust no one who answers the question.")

At a certain point in life, it becomes obvious that many if not most of our valued things will survive us; they suddenly seem innocent in their lack of consciousness and vulnerable in their durancey. We long to take better care of things that last, a curious devotedness given our startling temporality.

Benjamin's image is deservedly iconic, the Angel of History looks backward and what we see as the wind of progress, it sees as a storm of devastation. Yet I prefer Shakespeare's picture of little surrounded surfaces, our consciousness, the planet, the cosmos itself, "these banks and shoals of time" – bounded by an indifferent and eroding infinity.

Despite the creative potential of capitalism, the world is beginning to look like a bright labeled product past its sell by date. Despite?

Capitalism must expand to survive (Marx). Now that its scope is global, it must more intensely commercialize the intimate and the natural ; Segways, say, instead of walking.

The largest entrepreneurial continent is yet untouched. Brief, medically managed Near Death Experiences will be just the beginning.

The Aztecs rip out the hearts of captives to keep the universe wound up. The Spanish burn heretics to keep God happy. Apart from the fate of ordinary Indians, one takes satisfaction in the contestation of these cruel imperial elites; never have enemies better deserved each other. And yet there is a space for sympathy, apprehending their first meeting on the causeway to Tenoctitlan, the Spanish sick with desire seeing the natives so casually bedecked with gold, the Aztecs set to bestow on these dangerous strangers the thing they hold most precious -- gleaming cloaks made from turquoise feathers of the shy, the forest dwelling quetzal.

Who was more rational, the rapacious Spanish, retching from their visit to the blood encrusted temple, telling Montezuma he must accept Christ or that mild man replying "our gods have been good to us and we like them."

Sparrows see parked automobiles as shelter from sun in summer, snow in winter; moving they are dangers. They can't conceive the real meaning of "car", theirs a knowing nexus of needs and hazards. Our knowledge of the universe, even with the laws of physics, isn't much better.

The desire for life (action) and the desire for death (rest), these are the opposing weights that keep us ballasted and upright upon this spinning globe.

How often, feeling the wet wind and hearing the liquid sounds, it seemed to me the solution to every human grief and folly was in the falling rain.

We are not so much machines for remembering as processes for forgetting.

The most common moan: "If only I had known."

People have immense natural resistance to the recognition that they are often detestable. This is as it should be because the despicably self-aware are dangerous.

Describing kings with utter realism (a king is like everyone else except he eats better and sleeps worse), Shakespeare did more to undermine monarchy than Robespierre.

Instead of perambulating around Elsinore like a nocturnal tour guide, Old Hamlet as ghost needs do nothing more than haunt brother Claudius a few nights to make the usurper throw himself off a cliff or retire to a monastery, Gertrud untouched. But being a busy body (as ghosts tend to be), he has to spook Horatio, the guards, Hamlet Jr. and cause a lot of unnecessary deaths. Maybe he wants company. Maybe he enjoys the play.

The presentation of cruelty is sometimes a meditation on mercy.

My apparent mildness is due to intensities that cancel themselves out.

The disturbing thing about life isn't its brevity (in a life of normal span and social opportunity you can achieve all you need to) but its "temporality"; the entirety of people, places, projects, problems that meant so much at the time which from the lengthening track of your life seem like stations passed on an 'express-through' train, (and on every platform, your younger self thinking "my life is speeding by").

It's true, you don't have a real self, an enduring soul but no god has your perspective on the universe.

Taking yourself seriously is a service best performed by others.

The twenty year old bride and groom are looking at each other intensely, no smiles. I remember how she filled him up visually, he didn't even think of the problems already apparent, issues with sex, his envy of her energy and intelligence. These were white water, shallows, nothing to the force taking them out to the depths, the irreconcilable, the inconsolable.

In attempting to conceal the effect of your beauty, I most effectively communicated the effect of your beauty. (And knew I was doing so.)

What should be the usual evaluative standard for any object- "would even one person miss this if it didn't exist" doesn't apply to art because new art creates utterly unanticipable conditions for its need.

Artists create their art for the big audiences—the dead ("the used to live") and the unborn ("the yet to live"), hardly regarding that small minority, the currently living, excepting the artist himself. Artists always strive to please themselves, a fact relevant to the rest of us only insofar as that process was easy or hard.

Once the mourners are inside the church or chapel, the funeral company's driver and attendants light up and laugh. Given the nature of their business, this is entirely understandable and business is always good.

After the cat died, I adopted the phrase "not yet dead" for "living" as in "Is he still not yet dead?" or " I was not yet dead there for many years."

Fake out. It is possible to laugh at Death who destroys my body yet spares my work. In sports terms, the bonehead went for the man when he should have gone for the ball.

Silkworms in the five days of cocoon spinning must not be disturbed by any sudden loud sound that stops the intricate motions of their tiny heads. In the Spanish silk villages, where storms come up quickly, at the first rumble of distant thunder, the people would gather in the silk barns with pots, drums and songs, making a resemblingly joyful din as the storm intensified so that even thunder was just a patch in the sonic weave, the worms protected by a cocoon of sound, the silver thread unbroken.

If my book was designed to be a failure, who are you to call it one? The right term is success.

There is nothing like "the acknowledgements", the author's generous gesturing to assuage his selfishness, for gauging with no additional reading the extent of any book's hypocrisy and bad faith.

After two weeks of Fall's searing clarity, how one longs for a more hospitable season – winter's short days and sight lines, the difference between a lover/stranger's cruel candor and a friend's congenial hypocrisy.

There are events that give permanent shape to thought, one's brain is knocked into frame and events, distant in past and future, acquire relatedness and situation as if one were looking at a map, this the place of a still rancoring defeat, that the site of a beautiful cathedral, everything plotted along longitudes and latitudes of meaning.

The true aphorism is like a shy person at a party; all the talk makes it want to disappear.

The aphorism is so intensely verbal, one flees with relief to reading (or writing) a four hundred page novel. (The novel, the Academy painting of our era, false to life when it tries to be artful and false to art when it tries to be lifelike.)

He said "Your aphorisms remind me of used condoms." Tucked into the insult, I detected a kind of compliment.

Riddle. How is a book of aphorisms like a small town racetrack? *The same nags go round and round.*

Like that pledging sip of the sea one takes on the last day of vacation, our knowledge is a taste of hopeful brine.

Nothing is more awe inspiring than the exonerating self-regard of the guilty.

To a certain artist, not entirely fairly. No matter how you proliferate and torque them, your oblongs are just polygons, of no more interest than those dog turds that, in some circles, are bronzed and considered art.

The Dalai Lama wears shoes, participates in the marketplace's moral ambiguity of give and take, supply and demand. The karma of karma is economics.

"Joy is the feeling of reality" (Simone Weil). Yet the only indubitable thing is our pain. Not "cogito" (all our thoughts could be those of a green worm dreaming on Mars) but "Excrucior ergo sum."

Given the choice of a long comfortable life or a shorter one of stress and love, most of us would choose the latter because only love is worth the price of death.

_____ (fill in the blank), as sad as a drawer of ornithologically arranged hummingbirds.

In sex's long drawn game with death, individuals are the sacrificed pawns.

"No one gets through life without physical and emotional damages." Curious this platitude should be a consoling mantra. Granted, everyone looks good with medals and everyone deserves a decoration for showing up.

Traitors always have their reasons and sometimes they are good ones.

He had gotten ever lighter in his being, thin as paper, suitable then, for biography.

In art and sex we achieve our essential self-expression. Hence lies the non-biological fount of sexual jealousy – how dare you share your essential identity, reveal your code to another? The actual acts are nothing, light flickering on a page.

In relationships, what passes for fidelity is often mere misanthropy.

I realized I had done enough damage in this life, had fulfilled a negative moral quota and could, with a sense of satisfaction, turn towards the good.

It does seem the odds may have shifted in your favor once the worst has happened.

As to my former best friend, I haven't the slightest impulse to forgive or receive her forgiveness, which I am sure she feels also; four points of negativity that stake out the dead zone where I care more for a stranger in the obituaries than I do whether she lives or dies, a null point of absolute estrangement that can only be reached when the power of love is fully reversed. To think that with just a little more span of bitterness backwards, this might have become art.

They say every third drink (two are okay) takes ten minutes off your life. And this is drawn against what? – some future ruin of a man wishing he had a drink.

The twang of the literary always calls for a second glance since it usually emanates from a plucked chicken.

Hummingbirds sip sweetness from even a plastic flower.

"Which German city are we fire bombing today?" The good are easily damaged, committing wrongs to defeat evil. Evil people, doing the rare accidental good, are never improved. Such then is evil's power and why it must be fought even at the price of irremediable moral wounding.

It is always later than you think but the worst has already happened.

The problem, which is to say, the limitation of visual art is its apparency. Literature always has another dimension, that of its remove.

People really do resist all that happy self-realization; the serpent in the garden is in our hearts.

The young woman, lost at night in the new city, stands at the corner. If she turns right, she finds a directional sign; left, she meets a helpful stranger. The next morning, people get up for work, dress children for school. The local news: the world doesn't stop for one dead girl. Police are justified for another day.

All dicta need to be qualified with the briefest commentary: a question mark. (?)

We need to acknowledge things of darkness as our own. Even under our best illumination, we are objects in a world and cast shadows.

So many lives and ways of living, so many varieties of death matched to meet them.

I dropped a bomb of flattery and watched its low arching fall, penetrating the vessel through all its under decks with no outward sign of the deep hit until she was sinking, sinking in my arms.

Even the aphorism is contaminated by style.

I used to prefer bright autumn days, such possibilities. Now I prefer grey winter ones – such closures.

Those blank looks – everybody running their fluid consciousness over some stone of embedded sorrow, trying to smooth it down.

Our great modern cathedrals (airports and hospitals) aren't complete without the designers' afterthought, those little chapels where you never see anyone, spaces conceded to be wasted, over-invested even at mere meeting room size for those few times when one person needs to be alone.

Among the powers of the handsome is that of lying and being believed. Not much of victory for them or defeat for the duped since our natural bias sees the beautiful as the true. So much so that doubting the mendacious beauty is the false position, being allegiant to the "truth" of their falsity the true one. As Shakespeare notes, "She was beautiful, it would have been vicious to have mistrusted her."

Stones give meaning to the mortar.

Rochefoucauldian. Our sense of being honest with ourselves disables us for detecting deception in others, a curious thing since this sense of self-sincerity is itself a deceit.

The university's distinguished writer makes the expected pronouncement ... "Writing can't be taught" thereby communicating two things; he is a natural talent and his employment fraudulent.

Overcoming the tiger by riding it: not an option for the tiger.

As I observed in the workplace, oppression doesn't make people beautiful and revolutionary, it makes them mean, ugly and justifiable subjects for subjugation.

Hard to imagine that America was ever "fresh", that she was youthful at least until the nineteen-forties when her victory in the war (the only real victor) combined with the maturation of world wide media meant she became, from over-indulgence and overexposure, almost instantly more geriatric than Europe, lacking too "the old country's" archeological exhibitions of refinement.

Semi-asleep, what he heard as waves breaking on the shore was the wind raking the dry autumnal trees.

It is easy to find pride amid the accomplished. For real arrogance, you must locate the modest man who flinches at all admiration.

A dose of egotism can sometimes deacidify the corrosive effects of modesty. Humility, however, is beyond cure.

My recreational study was the vanquished, how even good preparation could turn on bad luck, resulting in lost battles, failed expeditions, disastrous engagements. So when my own defeat came, it shouldn't have been surprising. Why did I fight it long past the point of any outcome except substantial, self-inflicted injury? Because if it was my fate, it had to be authentic. It had to be unacceptable.

The basis of friendship is reciprocal aggrandizement, mutual affinity being its subtlest form. As in any construction, the foundation must not be exposed if the superstructure is to survive.

As Nietzsche observes, our freedom, demonstrated in choice, is essentially travel along predestined roads. Real freedom may only be manifest in reaction, what do we do in defeat, our responses to irremediable reverses. It is a common observation that the best writing occurs under tyranny. Our truest originality emerges when we are compelled to resistantly retreat from predilected paths of positivity; freedom as The Negative.

All lies are untruths but the only true lie is the one that is believed.

After many platitudinous steps, he stumbled over a profundity.

Survivors either are pulled back by the black gravity of the event into annihilating union, numbness and death or they desperately push themselves forward to make distance, with so little divagation and pause, it looks for all the world like focus and determination.

The only remedy for narcissism is the utterly unlooked for and unwanted event. Yet even catastrophe becomes in time a familiar chasm around which all the familiar mental furniture is arranged. For renewed perspective another application of disaster is required and so it goes. Toxic medicine of this kind is usually effective except that after "x" number of doses, there is nothing left (of the patient) to cure.

Remorse cannot ride upon success. It walks in the dust and may never catch up.

Adorno is wrong to say we only experience happiness in reflection. When we are happy, we know it. It is odd he doesn't make the more obvious observation: in remembering happiness we have a derived pleasure; remembering grief or sorrow, we experience the thing itself.

You can be sure a person is a friend when you begin to feel for them a gratuitous resentment.

We writers in short forms whatever our deficiencies have one virtue. We don't presume your patience.

I won't be able to take literature entirely seriously until it is possible to write backwards.

We intellectuals can easily dismiss the triteness, tiresomeness, the bland datedness and predictability of old TV and film. Yet we think contemptible those youth that feel similarly about our favorites of "essential art and literature." I recall taking a young doctor to an early music concert. She said "It all sounds too old to me" and has done decades of good work without benefit of Buxtehude.

The damage could never be repaired and so it resembled that other inexorable, relegating death from categorical singularity to an eventual and hopeful homeopathic cure both of itself and that living irremediable.

Never complain about an unfaithful lover. Everyone understands love is game of chance and no one wants to hear about a gambler's losses. In this area, cheaters appear nobler than complainers.

The inertial force of Time can propel us past our victories and defeats to a place reverse sloped to its leading indications where it's the victorious who experience angst, and the vanquished, untethered joy. That Time can does mean Time will. Generally we are dropped off at Acceptance-Resignation, a battlefield park where the descendents of old warriors (ourselves) visit the still valenced monuments – here a famous breakthrough, there a last stand.

My thoughts run on why not my sentences?

Apart from all the flux and flow, the rush of grey water and tempest, there remains an aquifer, deep, still, pure.

Nothing is more cheerful than watching chipmunks dart among the headstones.

At dawn, I don't want to get up. The cats, already up, wants to get out, a daily reminder that the world is an arena of competing urgent interests. Thanks for that, cat.

The odd asymmetrical symmetry of virtues and vices: in minor mode, "sins" are often virtues ("dishonesty" as courtesy and consideration) while excessive virtues are usually evil (the always honest man is cruel, etc.).

The defeated sometimes have the incomparable consolation of seeing the winners choke on the fruits of victory.

What a relief, looking up at the stars on a cold night and seeing they pattern no meaning. (The music of the spheres comes down to static.)

Philosophy of the horse race. The most handsome horse is not a good bet unless, by record, it is the best horse. And still it loses. So the next race, you go for the tough looking, at odds, plug – and the best horse wins. The irony being that this lesson, which can be learned stake free at the track, costs a great deal in life at large.

The demands of justice and the persuasions of pity are reconciled in the conclusion that people deserve to be loved, an obligation so far beyond our capacity to fulfill it, we necessarily pass it on to God whose most apparent characteristic is absence.

No one really dances with death but each of us is partnered with some deadening weight which in our efforts to stay upright gives a characteristic figuration to our motion, the choreography of life.

All night the thoughts drift down that in the morning I pin to the tree, dead leaves.

Night thoughts like torches; ashes in the morning.

The clinic is open on Christmas Eve (so many intestines, so little time) and being wheeled to the colonoscopy, I see off to the side a little room, a table set with chips and dip, cheeses, an unlit candle. Despite the embarrassments of digestion, the staff is rising to the occasion. They plan to eat.

After visiting my doctor, I am always resolved to live more fully and forcefully. This is a routine of my reliably boring life.

For all the good America has done, it is going to pay for its production and promulgation of stupidity, the way Africa paid for ritual, Europe for pride, Asia for tradition. In a just universe, it will pay as a just consequence; in a natural one, as a natural result. Nature never forgives stupidity.

The only way he could be true to himself and to truth was by lying. Consistent dishonesty was a form of sincerity. (This isn't about me.)

The city and the country are both shown to be corrupted in Shakespeare's creepy comedies, The Merchant of Venice and Twelfth Night. The "feel-good" positive of the lovers' resolution appears very shallow set against the irremediable humiliations of Shylock and Malvolio, men set loose in the world like hurt furies to make more misery.

The magazine describes mules as "honest." Of course, with comically credulous ears, a long patient face with guileless brown eyes, the practical tubular body on sturdy knobby legs, ungainly, willing, capable – the very icon of honesty, the mule.

Our capacity for victimhood is a kind of talent. It insists on being developed.

Is "green grief" not a phrase? It should be, for the kind not dry, set or hardened that's supple, growing, full of sap.

All of us are "walking wounded". In time the deduction is obvious enough: no wounding, no walking.

My best thoughts were expressed in sex, with the usual problematics of translation – that the erotics were good didn't mean the thoughts were.

If our skins suddenly became transparent we would be transfixed with pity and horror at the garish congestion of organs and for a week might be careful and kind.

He congratulated himself on his integrity, not having a single friend.

Wise men say: keep your deepest grief to yourself, don't burden others or belittle it in utterance, weakening its utility as a dark energizer. This deep grief, the fundamental tender of your personal economic system, circulated in the foreign country of an indifferent world, is revealed to be just another bit of engraved memory – "one thousand Pangs", "ten million Hurts", as preposterously inflated and undervalued as Weimar Marks or Zimbabwean dollars.

Except for sentimental war-vet festivals and a proprietal piety for our immediate genealogy, we have no regard for our ancestors (all of humanity) who loved, worked and suffered to give us our world nor do we much care for those who will inherit the future, otherwise we'd make better personal and environmental provision for them. Fair enough; the already dead and the not yet born hardly have a thought for us. Everyone's province is the pressured and impassioned present; the past and the future only exist as egoistical projections of our memory and desire. And we do not believe we will die.

We begin our lives as children and should we live so long, having passed through the fury of our bodies, we become children with knowledge, congratulating ourselves on our survival and calling it wisdom. Not that we've gotten the answers; we've stopped asking the questions.

Dreams are thoughts thinking.

3AM, the worst time, the luminous clock hands form a stationary right angle, a coal scoop containing doubt, remorse, frustrations, mopes. It's too late to stay up and too early to rise, one is pinned like a specimen bug. Ah, the hand has moved – one minute closer to dawn.

The captain's "ten commandments" were mostly what you'd expect – no drinking on duty, no smoking below decks, etc. But– "Anyone fighting in the lifeboats will be shot and thrown overboard." astounded me; the punishment was so harsh and why did he think we'd ever be in lifeboats when our ship was so large, modern and well-manned?

Literary ambitions, successes, people, agents, reputations, conversation, grants, news, prizes, events, criticism, in every instance the operative adjective may be supplanted by "embarrassing."

The fat but not unintelligent king's favorite indoor activity, aside from eating and drinking, is assembling locks and fitting keys as if sympathetic-magically, he will get better at inserting his personal clef in Marie Antoinette's personal lock, as if a doubly assertive turn might at once unlock the complexities of state and secure the royal future. Fumble on – the Switzers still guard the gates and lacy lawyers are thinking reform.

We should meditate fifteen minutes a day on why we are disliked and the justice of our enemies. Comprehending these antipathies is more redemptive than prayer.

Eventually, you learn certain things can't be coped with; that's how they are coped with.

Since all us carry weight, we can overthrown ourselves, the weight becoming impetus; one is simultaneously victor and vanquished. This aesthetic judo is called *art*. The hardest thing about it is the first thing, getting a firm grip on oneself.

Style is not an indulgence but a transcript of fate.

The minute I became slightly wise I became totally silent. That was how I knew.

Gardeners are murderers if weeds are as innocent as flowers.

Decades ago, William Stafford wrote "In Oregon, the best poets are still the coyotes." Nothing has much changed except coyotes now howl in every contiguous state.

We were never meant for paradise, not backwards (Eden) or forward (heaven), a fact acknowledged by our deep allegiance to things we knock into shape, for engines that need to be kicked before they run.

With eons of non-existence before and after us, our lives are as brief as fireflies on a summer night. They have matured and mate in a dance of lights. Maybe they appreciate the beauty of it, maybe not; we have no idea of what it is like to be a firefly. But their lives are not too short for them. Nor ours, if we have worked, loved and made what light we can.

Here lies the aphorism, an epitaph of thought.

Writer's cramp. He felt pressured, all his books having to be written under the harshest deadline, their needing to be finished before he got bored with them which always happened on the first page.

Whenever I am ill or fear death, I have feelings of forgiveness towards everyone who has harmed me. When healthy, I harbor thoughts of revenge. The reverse should be the case. If the injury was so great, one might reasonably want retribution to the very end, while in the fullness of one's powers, surely there is no better way to live than in an ever expanding frame of caring, compassion and consideration.

The last lesson taught me by my cat: don't complain about dying.

"I am tired of my little stories, like birds bred in cages". Katherine Mansfield.

Lexical Rights Advisory. Readers aggrieved by consumption of previously appearing propositions may have right of compensatory recourse under the following terms and conditions. Complaint parties should specify prior encountered statements by page and placement in the author's already published books, Compensation will be awarded at the rate of one cent (U.S.) per repeated aphorismic unit on a onetime, one recipient basis, subject to a fifty cent (U.S.) deduction for processing and handling. While made "in good faith", the above tender does not constitute a contract, guarantee, redemption or promise to pay in the legal sense and establishes no obligation, moral or fiduciary, on the author who is the sole arbiter of all claims and of any dispute arising therefore and with all normal and customary privileges of non-compliance. This offer, herein know as "the offer", as and if iterated, replicated or reproduced is not itself a referent object under terms of "the offer." Claims may be made, via email, including notarized electronic signature and federal tax filing number to: Egent4@hotmail.com. Or sent in writing to 1641 Rugby Ave, Charlottesville, Va 22903, USA, close to one of the original locations Jefferson considered for the University of Virginia, and near the city's highest elevation in the historic Rugby area, "1641"commemorating the year of the signing of The Great Remonstrance, is a cottage style residence in the Petit Trianon manner that blends naturally with the existing, unspoiled landscape and designer built-environment found on picturesque Rugby Avenue. A sophisticated dwelling embracing Old World charm and modern conveniences, this is a coveted residential situation. Unique in age and amenities, possessing commodious interior and exterior spaces for relaxation and entertaining, with rustic elements and classic post war lines, vintage elegance is the resonant note. Craft-fabricated ash block walls with antique over-painting, and hand-poured concrete foundation, plank floors, vintage moldings, luminous fenestrations, all project the warmth for a relaxed and refined abiding. Listed in Tolkien's Register of Virginia Homes, Huts and Habitations.[75] Offer expires 9/1/2017.

---

75 "East of Rugbydale, the last homely hovel. Occupied (1955) by Alf (grocer) and Elfie Elrond."

Donated Poetry

I am grateful to the following friends, associates and one former partner who have generously contributed the sequent poems and helped underwrite publication costs of *Laminations*.

THE POETS and BENEFACTORS

Calvin ("Cal") Collins is America's foremost practitioner and advocate of the New Poetree. The recipient of every significant honor for poetry, he is Dean for Life of the Council of Contemporary Poetry, a permanent tenure afforded only one other occupant (Charles Borestein). After four decades of writing, teaching, mentoring and conventioneering, Cal is tirelessly devoted to the recognition of young talent and the expansion of linguistical possibility. (The above was graciously supplied by the Outreach Presidium of the Council of Contemporary Poetry)

Victory in Overtime

Spice bottles in leaf it is stop and go until. Halts, of course, along the Green Line.
If the horizon supplied, it was typical capital expansion. When the wind rose on Tuesday.
She never advocated that not in a black raincoat. Histories of seldom said so.
"You just can't be too sure, can you?" = Verona, oranges in the market,
Names that made steam. The invasion was billed big screen,
              Only it was.

Emily Louise Brooks worked for many years as an admission officer for the University of Virginia's Curry School of Education and served for twenty-five years in the United States Air Force reserve. This is her first published poem since college.

A clatter of orders, complaintive armies rouse,
heavyweights' stagger, blows.
Tomorrow, snakes of crooked smoke,
hollowed out days, husks of hope.
Swept clean, time's scrape on slate
until comes that coldest clearest moon
glinting metal scraps, bits of bone,
a detection of stars (how much she knows).
The next night forgets all – white out
snow on snow, deepest pall.

Phillip Ferguson is Cataloger and Registrar for Boston University art museums. With Lisa Roth, he is author of *Art Object Registry, a Modern Method* that in the decade since initial publication has become the recognized standard of practice for the profession. Phil writes poetry in his spare time, what he calls his "fullest time", with poems published in *Antiphon*, *Agni*, *The Virginia Quarterly Review*, and other venues. "My ideal job would be with *The Daily Racing Form* using my analytic skills to study thoroughbred performances and then writing the little post race précis; "Wind Storm started slow but came on, challenging in the stretch, stalled, four lengths back, placed."

Cracks in the Enamel

The weekend
my left bicuspid shattered
I was emailed the news –
"Have you heard?
Your friend Ed is dead."

As I probed the jagged,
gummy stump.
the pain and void
my tongue revealed
was him, or his.

And when I thought
of absolute loss,
it was that tooth
(of which I was fond)
I kept focusing on.

So, were my nerves
of mourning crossed?
And was that bad?

A reflective gentleman
sit across from me on the T.
Dim eyed, sunk cheeked,
he rubs his face. Twitchy
with age or teething a grief,
the only one to ask.

———————————

Sidney Sussex was born in Stratford Ontario and attended McGill University and St John's College, Cambridge. After a varied career in critical journalism, he is currently Arts Editor for The Toronto Star. Author of one novel, *A Masque of Revels* and two books of poetry, *Inquisitions* (1999) and *Changing Lanes* (2007, short-listed for the 2008 Governor's Generals Prize), he cultivates a strictly indigenous species garden midway between Guelph and Toronto.

The crows' inquisitorial calling,
the only flaw in the inexpressible light.
"What?" "When?"
The usual interrogations, queasy exonerations.
A wail of "whys" unwinding
universes split at a shift of glance, a shuffle of atoms,
in other whirls, billions of universes, billions of yous.
and not one where you aren't guilty or in doubt.
Otherwise, they can't be you.

Jamail aka **J.J. Jones** was born in Hampton Virginia and educated at Virginia Commonwealth University. He co-founded and is lead bassist /song writer for the Rap-HipHop Fusion group Streetap which has fronted for Kobey, Purple, IMTALKINGTOU and other top bands. He owns /manages Blacktracks, a recording studio that has debuted regional and national talents like Tyrone White, Felonious Hawkes and Man Stuff. A book of his lyrics and poetry is forth coming. Jamail supports "Equal Economics."

What's cooking in the spoon's half full moon
Shines, takes the grim off the road's hard dime,
Mean streets where accidents happen.
Man, in yo brain's feta cheese, face recognition
Throngs. At the line up, cakewalk, perp-talk
You always get it wrong. Death row, death slow.
End of the line. Turn on the juice.
Let it shine shine shine.

Esteemed as our foremost new wave feminist poet and "a force to be reckoned with" (Don Chaissen, The New Yorker), **Emily Motes** or **Queenrain** is a much sought after commentator, performer, reciter and lecturer. Recipient of an Academy of American Poets Trailblazer Award, a Guggenheim grant and numerous other honors, she is author of ten books of poetry and open action plays,(*Soap and Water, Bug Bear, The Sadness of Saddles, A New Fuk, Dream Tote, Now Isn't, Not Me But You, Wrench, Screw*) including, *Woman Overboard*, Winner of the 2014 Goldsmith Prize. Queenrain teaches at The New School, New York

I hate your crap. Stop the computer tap.
burn your paper cell. Try honest work.
god I hate WASPs, no sing, broken stings.
no honey in your hives. Stocks of bonds.
oppressors of all kinds, your day is done.
imagine. No more haves, have nots.
try stopping a thousand flowers bloom,
colors, queers, weirds are thrusting up
fuck you wasps. You need it up the ass.
but are afraid to ask. Answer this:
who oppressed you?

Paul Patroone was born in Litchfield England and educated at Manchester University. After a round the world tour following graduation, Patronne studied oriental religions in Dharamsala and Pusan before moving to the United States, teaching at Naropa, Antioch, Baxter, and other American universities. The author of over fifty books and chapbooks, Patroone directs courses in literature, poetics and the history of religions via Uncle Ezra's Electronic University (www.UncleEzra#.edu). He owns a small ranch near Learcliffe, Montana and is listed 67th in *Google-Poetry Today's* ratings of the most reclusive poets in America.

"Who cares what happened to them? In literature we require distinction, charm, beauty and imaginative power."
Oscar Wilde, *The Decay of Lying.*

Canto One.
Dear Joe and Josephine Poet,
whether you write in scannable feet and common forms
or take tradition by the horns, (another tradition)
no one wants to hear about your woes and foes,
loves won and lost, your despair or the color of her hair,
death of the heart, late night with tarts,
your experiences as a child, walks in the wild.
No one cares if you are black, white or stripped.
You views are not news. Your verse won't fix the planet,
    must less the pipes.
There's zero value in your verbal quirks.
Unless you are a Shakespeare, Donne or Dickinson
do us a favor, shut the fuck up.

Canto Two
Why doesn't it make you sick, your new, selected, elected
your greatest and latest, your OUP collated confected.
The blown-up blurbs about your words.
Nobody cares about your blues and screws, your always
　about your news.
Sure we get it, language speaks thru us, we are
　mouthpieces,
our voices aren't our own, somewhere a muse has flown.
But can't you see you're a little terrier with his tail stuck up,
doing his tough guy strut. Yak-Yak-Yak . Me, I'd rather
　hear a tomcat moan.
　　　　　And I'm no lady cat.

William Ruminant holds advanced degrees from the University of Virginia and Yale. From 1996 to 2015 he was director of the William Ruminant Institute of Textual Studies (WRITES) at Edmister University. The author of *After the Fire* (OUP), *Pretext: a manual for editing in the postmodern era* (Harvard) and numerous scholarly articles, he is Senior Docent in English at the University of Singapore. *Distempered : an academic biography* will be published next year (Verso.)

My Beautiful Career
A building of honest brick and modern design,
the carpets, blue steel teal; accentual wood.
Lighting, indirect, a few brass lamps for their cultivated
　gleam.

The students were subservient-keen, my colleagues each
   mastered a garden.
And I the genial sun, grown large and generous. There
   was no danger there.
Then I made a mere mistake, of the human all too
   humankind kind.
Suddenly the wolf was out, all the wolves, the pack.
They gobbled me up. Blood and guts.

Carolyn Frost is Rita May Dove Professor of English at Radford University. She is the author of seven books of poetry and *The Gathering Wind*, a critical study (co-authored with Lyndall Brown) on the reception of Emily Dickinson in the last decades of the nineteenth century. She also directs the Blue Ridge Writers' Retreat, Radford, Virginia.

After
Those dying phlox polished by moonlight and wind
As if to scour from portal and window an illumination:
   later
A kind of cry and quick ululation
Down the scale a species and fields away
Summer's dew jewels, crystals on the rose lips
Focus the wet light into liquid yearning
For the half lived, discarded syllables, moments
Dropping in my dry defoliated heart what was before

Page Nelson received a full scholarship to attend the University of Virginia, from which he was subsequently expelled. Drifting into librarianship, he concluded his career as Technical and Reference Librarian at Harvard's Graduate School of Design. He is the author of four chapbooks of poetry and five volumes of literary mixed media (see *Page Nelson: a checklist* compiled by graduate students of the Bowers Bibliographical Seminar (2015), University of Virginia, Department of English).[76] His most significant contribution to culture was his suggesting the fastening stubs be moved to the fore edge (opposing spine side) on a prototype book protection box being demonstrated by Library of Congress technicians in 1978. Design specifications with this improvement were subsequently distributed to libraries, to become, manufactured in studio and commercially, the worldwide "first resort" measure for book preservation ... (*edited for brevity*).

---

76 The 2015 seminar was taught by Antonin Kershberg (who replaced William Ruminant); enrolled students received three course-hour credits.

Postscriptomb

On the last night (Aug. 22, 2016) before forwarding this manuscript to my publisher, I was reading D.J. Taylor's *The Prose Factory: literary life in England since 1918* and encountered this sentence: "Frederica Potter's (a character in A.S. Byatt's 2002 novel *A Whistling Woman*) own first work, *Laminations*, is another scrupulous reflection of prevailing tastes: an example of the fashionable 1960s preoccupation with cut and paste collage: an attempt not to pursue the old Forsterian idea of connectedness but to insist on the advantages of separation and disengagement." *Plus ca change.*

Since even with an average mind, I can envision and endorse a critic's view that this book's journal entries are suffocating; infelicitous in their conveyances (style) and what they convey (content), that the poetry is prosaic, and the dicta commonplace, it is not unreasonable to hope that a superior person will detect features or flickering fireflies of interest unadvocable [sic?] by the author. Facetiousness, for all its falseness, is a kind of freshness that Time develops, like photographic chemistry, into the stuff of fact.